iMOODivate

· · · · · · ●●●●●●●●●●●● · · · · ·

Dramatically Improve Your Life in Just
Six Seconds a Day and Not All at Once

JAY CUMMINGS

Copyright © 2021 Jay Cummings

All rights reserved. No part of this book may be reproduced, stored, or transmitted by any means—whether auditory, graphic, mechanical, or electronic—without written permission of both publisher and author, except in the case of brief excerpts used in critical articles and reviews. Unauthorized reproduction of any part of this work is illegal and is punishable by law.

CONTENTS

Dedication 5
Foreword 7
Introduction 11

Chapter 1:   Tom Murphy 13
Chapter 2:   First Encounters 27
Chapter 3:   Energy (My Superpower) 32
Chapter 4:   Dave 42
Chapter 5:   Allison 45
Chapter 6:   Dan 54
Chapter 7:   Tribute: Loren Poirier 59
Chapter 8:   Mitch Durfee 64
Chapter 9:   My First Nosedive in MOOD 71
Chapter 10: Those Negative Ninnies 77
Chapter 11: It's Not What's in the Cards You've
                Been Dealt, It's How You Play Them ... 84
Chapter 12: The Great Race 92
Chapter 13: Skinning 98
Chapter 14: COVID 103

Chapter 15: Close of Business............................113
Chapter 16: Six Seconds a Day
 (and Not All at Once) 122

About the Author...127

DEDICATION

As a small-town motivational speaker, there are several anecdotes I use to inspire event attendees to take action. One example: 'A year from now, you'll wish you had started today!' Another one, in Yogi Berra fashion, 'Nothing happens until something happens.' Meaning get off your ass and take some action. But perhaps the best quote used in these scenarios is 'It's the *start* that *stops* most people.' Let that sink in a bit.

I cannot tell you the number of years that went by while the book I'd intended to write remained unwritten. I thought of book idea after book idea to no avail. Then I felt compelled to take action on *this* topic; the one that I feel so strongly about. But I'd have never taken that first step if it weren't for my coworker, one month before she retired, agreeing to help me write a book. 'Kerry, want to write a book with me?' I fired off in an email. To my surprise, she immediately and enthusiastically accepted!

Let's say that Kerry Deschamps and I have little in common, and it would have been easy for me to dismiss her and continue on with my life. What a mistake that would have been! What opportunities would have been missed? It would have been very small-minded of me to not get to know Kerry. At first, in conversations, she would leave a small piece of information that prompted me to question my beliefs. I took the nugget, thought about it, evaluated and reevaluated it, and if it stayed with me, I'd put it in my quiver for future use. More often than not, I accepted and adopted the new information. Even the ideas that I disagreed with, I kept and continued to evaluate as I knew that Kerry simply saw things differently than I, and it was just going to take me some time to understand what she was saying.

Kerry is another great example of the lessons in this book. The universe is putting people or concepts in front of you and it's far too easy and comfortable to dismiss those that don't mirror your own beliefs. So, I ask you to look deep within your network; whose skills, talents or attributes are you overlooking? You do so at your own peril.

It took decades of having done *nothing*…. until Kerry, ever so skillfully, motivated me in the subtlest of ways to take action and write this book. A lifelong dream that nearly went unfulfilled was achieved with the help of a person outside my inner circle.

Kerry, thank you for tolerating me and my shenanigans; for supporting me, motivating me, and for doing the heavy lifting to help make this book a reality. This literally could not have been done without you. And for this you have my unconditional respect. With peace and gratitude.

FOREWORD

By: Patrick Decelles

When Jay asked me to write the foreword to his first book, I was beyond grateful and truly honored to do so. I have had the pleasure of knowing Jay since 1997, and since that first meeting, we have forged a genuine friendship based on mutual respect, shared affection, and personal admiration.

In addition to being one of my closest friends and favorite humans, Jay is one of the most humble, thoughtful, well meaning, well read and well-spoken people I've ever known. And though it may be an overused colloquial term in our part of the world, Jay Cummings is the real deal. With that said, he genuinely cares – OR, if you prefer to use his terminology – he clearly "gives a shit" about everyone with whom he comes into contact. And, if you ever get the chance to meet Jay in person, you will come to know that in less than six seconds - GUARANTEED!!!

As a self-described over-thinker, something that most of us can relate to, Jay is literally consumed by his concern for other people and how his words and actions will impact them. And, I believe that his desire to "leave his mark on the world" – with this how-to guide to better connection and more positive relating – stems from his heightened awareness of and keen sensitivity to other people's energy.

As you will read in the pages to follow, Jay's life up to this point in time has been one in which he has continuously strived to find the meaning in the things that he has experienced – both personally and professionally – and value the opportunities to learn from the people that have crossed his path. Out of that wealth of "life stuff," Jay has constructed a simple template for people to find meaning and become positive disruptors in their own lives – in just six seconds.

In so doing, those who decide to choose their mood each and every day – and, who then extend themselves with courage and confidence to share their mood-word – will not only enhance the quality of their lives but will also make a positive impact on the lives of those with whom they interact. Sounds simple, right? It truly is simple, and as I've grown older and hopefully wiser, I've come to understand and appreciate the fact that simplicity is profound and life changing.

In the end, if you make the daily commitment to this simple task and become a consistently positive disruptor and iMOODivator – dedicating yourself to creating a 6-second habit in all of your personal interactions – your life will profoundly change for the better. As Jay points out, you may have to fake it until you make it. Know this… if you read the book with intention and adopt his recommended 6-second practice as your own, you will be forever grateful for the information to follow. Welcome to the iMOOD-ivation movement!!!

INTRODUCTION

You have the power to make the single biggest change in your life. And it only takes seconds - or even a fraction of that.

I have discovered the twelve best answers to the most asked question on the planet.

(Now your brain is intellectually confounded. You want to know what the twelve best answers are, but you don't even know what the question is!)

The question is: How are you?

It's the most asked question on planet Earth, but it's given the least amount of interest. The least amount of consideration. The least amount of thought. How many times have you seen, heard, or participated in the mindless exchange of "How are you?" "Good, 'n' you?" without giving it a second thought? Perhaps millions!

We'll discuss why in greater detail later on, but right now I'm going to give you—in no particular order—the top twelve best answers to the most asked question on Earth!

- **Amazing**
- **Exceptional**
- **Fantastic**
- **Phenomenal**
- **Fabulous**
- **Incredible**
- **Magnificent**
- **Unbelievable**
- **Spectacular**
- **Awesome**
- **Beautiful**
- **Happy**

CHAPTER ONE

Tom Murphy

If you're like me, you skipped the introduction. In this case the introduction is the basis of the entire book, so if you did skip it, I urge you to take a minute to read it.

Though I said "in no particular order," there's a reason why I listed *amazing* first. Enter Tom Murphy.

Murphy is a six-foot-four former professional mixed martial arts fighter. Ripped. Solid muscle. Arms the size of my legs. He speaks with a hint of a Southern NYC/Philadelphia accent. Murphy's a rare individual. When you first meet him, he is in your face, overpowering, excitedly intrusive, making you feel slightly uncomfortable. He is fast-talking and passionate, beaming with optimism. He's larger than life and displays confidence that might be mistaken for arrogance. There's a twinkle in his eye and a smile on his face. Shy, he is not.

The first couple of times I met Murphy, I didn't really care for him. Something about him challenged me, and I was not sure how to react. He seemed over the top. In subsequent meetings, though, I learned that he is the real deal. He's like an army tank rolling toward you: you'll either get on board or be run over, but that's how he displays his passion for excitement. Murphy loves living life, and I don't know anyone living a fuller life than he. He'll present a project or concept by exclaiming, "We can change the world!" He's done that, and continues to do so. And I don't feel that he's even scratched the surface - he's just getting started. Whatever the cause, he immerses himself in it, finds a method to excel, and then watch out . . . he's off and running.

Oddly, he and I were probably two of the least book-smart people in our respective high schools. His SAT score was an even 500, and he had always been on the lookout for his equal. I edged him out with an embarrassing 820. Somehow, we both kicked it into high gear in college (yes, we got accepted) and graduated with honors.

We attended different schools and did not meet until 2009, but interestingly, we applied a similar technique to succeed: white-knuckled hard work. On the first day of college, I realized how much I *didn't* know. I understood my reason for being there, yet I did not have a foundation to build from. Goofing off throughout my first three years of high school had finally caught up to me, and I had to play catch-up.

So I resorted to the one thing I *did* know, and I didn't look back. I knew the value of hard work.

I was always a worker. During the summers of high school and the gap year before college, I worked my butt off. I framed houses during the day, from 8:00 a.m. to 4:00 p.m., rushed home, ate dinner, slept from 6:00 p.m. to 10:00 p.m., then worked the night shift stocking shelves at the Grand Union from 11:00 p.m. to 7:00 a.m. I then rushed home, ate breakfast, and headed back out to the construction job; repeat. In college, I applied the same killer work ethic. I went to the library after dinner, from 6:00 p.m. to 11:00 p.m., and did all my homework in each subject—each daily homework assignment—three times *each*, every night, Monday through Sunday. Eventually, because of the repetitive process, I simply started memorizing the work, and then it started making sense. Lasting comprehension soon followed. I graduated summa cum laude with a degree in computer programming.

Tom Murphy's strategy was similar. He sat in the front row of lecture halls, hanging on the professors' every word. He relentlessly asked questions until he understood. He once overheard this conversation between two professors in the teacher's lounge at his college. The first professor complained, "I've got this annoying student, sits in the front row. He's six foot four—a gigantic kid—who stares at me and asks question after question. It's so annoying."

The second professor chuckled. "Oh, that's Murphy. He reminds me of myself when I was young.

He's passionate, more so than the other students who aren't paying any attention at all."

The conversation gave the first professor insight into Murphy's learning style. He began treating Murphy as the star student. That tactic proved successful for both Murphy and the complaining professor.

***

Tom Murphy owns a local, highly successful restaurant with fifty employees, but that is his *part-time* job. Yup, running the restaurant is something he does for fun, in his "spare" time. His primary job is that of superhero.

Murphy founded *Sweethearts and Heroes*, an organization that explains and demonstrates to students and teachers the science behind bullying and how to eradicate it. Murphy has presented to over two million students from Maine to Hawaii to Canada. I caught my first glimpse of his feature presentation at a local high school.

Before I describe what Sweethearts and Heroes is as an organization, let me explain what the name means. It's not just a unique, catchy phrase that hipsters might come up with. Everything Murphy does has significant purpose. The name dates back to the 1500s, where a *bully* was actually your sweetheart, or a term of endearment. Back then, a bully was a defender; someone who'd look out for you. As this chapter unfolds, you will see how the organization's name, Sweethearts and Heroes, is a perfect name for what they do and how they do it.

My wife is an elementary school teacher, so I invited her along as an educated advisor. We sat in the auditorium with about four hundred students and a couple-dozen staff members, waiting for the assembly to begin. Finally, the lights dimmed. On a large screen at the head of the auditorium, a video showed Murphy, years earlier, fighting in a cage in Las Vegas in front of thousands of screaming fans. I knew Murphy was an MMA fighter, but I'd never *seen* him fight. I was initially stunned. The students' attention was immediately drawn to the match. They collectively oohed and aahed during the short highlight reel clip. Murphy and his opponent were competing, and it was rough. A couple of good hits landed, and blood spewed. At the end of the bout, Murphy's hand was raised as he was declared the winner. "*TOM MURPHY!*" the announcer bellowed over the packed stadium. Just then, the lights in the school auditorium were turned up; Murphy ran from the back of the room, down the center aisle, and took the stage, front and center, larger than life.

"Hi, everyone! My name is Tom Murphy, and I— hate— fighting!"

BOOM!

The students pointed at the video screen that had since gone black. Over the commotion, they yelled to their friends, "Wait, WHAT??" It was a trap to lure in the staff and students. They knew he was there to talk about bullying, and many confused fighting with bullying. Students were certain this was a "gotcha" moment.

In response, Murphy said, "Oh you mean that?" He jerked his thumb back over his shoulder toward the screen behind him. "Let me educate you on MMA. It's a sport, with two equally-balanced competitors of the same physical size and ability; and a referee. Medical staff and judges are there to ensure a safe, even match. It's not *fighting*; it's sport. Now, I'm not here to tell you that you have to like it, but to educate you on what it is and what it is not. I won't bring it up again.

"I hate fighting, and I've *never* gone into the ring with the intention of hurting another person." At that point, the image on the screen changed to a Norman Rockwell painting. It showed a big kid with his finger in the face of a much smaller kid. The smaller kid looked terrified. "I'm here to talk about bullying." You could have heard a pin drop in the auditorium. The audience was hooked.

Nearly half of the school principals that Murphy approaches sneer when he asks them to schedule ninety minutes for his presentation. Some have asked him if he was crazy. "You're going to keep the attention of ninth and tenth graders for an hour and a half? Good luck!" they say sarcastically.

That's when Murphy clarifies that he'll actually need an hour and *forty-five* minutes to complete the presentation properly. Some administrators have dismissed the request, mistaking Murphy for an uneducated wannabe with no idea how to keep the attention of students that age. Other administrators agree, but vow to themselves that they'd be there to step in when the kids acted out, as they inevitably would. Murphy knows he will rock the auditorium based on the hundreds of times he's done this before.

But this is no ordinary presentation. Principals become as awe-struck as the students. Murphy will admit that the MMA bout at the outset is a circus trick; it sets the hook to reel the audience in.

Murphy speaks the uncensored truth, based in scientific fact. Teachers and students are initially stunned, then become drawn in. Murphy says the secret to engaging kids—especially from the sixth- to twelfth-grade level—is to speak the truth. No sugar-coating here. The students are appreciative because they're not being coddled. They are getting the raw truth about bullying—why bullying happens and what the consequences are. Murphy offers a series of examples.

Bullying, coupled with the hopelessness it creates, has greatly contributed to the uptick in childhood suicide. Yup, kids are dying as a result. In 2018, deaths by suicide among ten- to fourteen-year-olds ranked second to accidents and surpassed childhood cancers.[1] View it this way for more of an impact: this increase in deaths is by their own hands. It's astonishing that in the present day, the most technologically advanced time in human history, we are losing ground on this near-epidemic situation.

---

[1] www.cdc.gov/nchs/fastats/child-health.htm

During the video portion of his presentation, Murphy projects a photo of a teenager who not only killed herself, but who broadcast her death in real time on social media. She fell victim to the true definition of bullying—the perpetual, habitual intent to harm someone repetitively, whereby others are recruited to help. Few know how to talk about this stuff, but Murphy explains the dynamics of bullying in such a manner that audiences are moved by their newfound understanding and want to help eradicate the problem. The students are then taught how to combat bullying, using what Murphy's organization calls *bystander empowerment*. Murphy's philosophy is this: a witness is in the best position to stop bullying in its tracks. A bystander's action is the key to stopping not only the current bullying activity but also future bullying.

Murphy believes that anyone who witnesses bullying can avert it more than 60 percent of the time by playing the superhero. What is a superhero? Sweethearts and Heroes defines it as someone who will do something that others will not, for example, springing into action when bullying is observed. Murphy says it's the stop, drop, and roll of bullying. Murphy then displays on the screen the famous quote by Albert Einstein. "The world is a dangerous place, not because of evil people, but because those of us who choose to do nothing about it!"

During his presentation, he asks the crowd to raise their hand if they know what to do when they catch on fire. The vast majority of kids raise their hands, and several belt out "STOP, DROP and ROLL!" Then Murphy asks the audience, "What do you do when you see someone being bullied?" Crickets. Maybe one hand raises and a person says hesitantly, "Tell a teacher?" They do not know. Murphy then asks, "What are the odds you'll catch on fire today?" The answer is very close to zero. To drive home his point, he asks, "What are the odds you will see bullying or be bullied today?" The answer is nearly 100 percent. Murphy wraps it up perfectly: "So for the thing that will *not* happen today, you all know exactly what to do, yet, for the thing that almost certainly *will* happen, you have no plan of action." Then, to some school staffs' dismay, he adds, "There are posters all over the walls of this school that claim zero tolerance for bullying; school rules prohibit bullying, and some states have anti-bullying laws, making it *illegal*, yet not one student in this school knows what to do in the face of bullying! That's why I am here—to give you a plan, to teach you what to do when you see bullying." Throughout most of the presentation, Murphy creates numerous interactions that challenge the students' and staff's perception. The problem needs to be examined from a different point of view. Murphy explains and then demonstrates to the staff and students his training methods to stop bullying. He calls this method the ABC's of Bullying:

- A = Away: bring the person away from the environment.

- B = Be their friend. Step in, and for example say, "Hi, 'Joe,' let's go to the gymnasium."
- C = Confront or call for help. Self-explanatory.

Murphy then asks the audience for volunteers. Three students are selected. Murphy explains to the volunteers that to be a superhero, you first need your superhero costume. He dresses the students up rather silly, with colored, rubberized swimming caps, swimming goggles, and of course a superhero cape. Murphy then sets up a "bully drill" prompting the students to take action. Murphy plays the part of the bully, wearing a mean-looking mask and hat. He begins each bully drill modeling his favorite superhero, Mr. Incredible, by looking straight into the audience and saying "Show Time!" After each drill, they do a quick review of it. By the end of the bully drills, the students have practiced each one of the ABC's of bulling. As you can imagine there are a lot of laughs and silliness, but Murphy's presentation evokes many different levels of awareness. It's a production his audience will not soon forget. And that's the point: to be top of mind. The presentation ends on a high note.

After the productions, students do one of two things: they either approach Murphy for a closer look at his massive, muscular physique, and maybe pose with him for a selfie. They share a high-five and then disburse.

Then there are the lingerers, who wait patiently to speak with Murphy privately. His presentation has resonated with them, and now, for the very first time, they feel understood. They feel a connection.

When I attend presentations, these are the kids I watch for. I wait on the opposite side of the auditorium, a hundred or more feet away, to allow them their privacy. They share their stories with Murphy. Tears and hugs follow. Murphy understands these kids and knows their situations. He has seen and heard it hundreds of times before. He lets them talk, then asks a question or two to strengthen the connection. The common thread of their messages is, "I'm that kid on the edge of doing something harmful to myself, and you gave me hope."

Occasionally, Murphy receives messages from kids that are too shy to come forward after a presentation. Here is a scaled-down version of one message Murphy shared with me:

> Mr. Murphy,
>
> I want to thank you for your presentation today. I had planned to kill myself after school today, but your presentation has given me hope. Thank you!

Other messages are less dire:

> Mr. Murphy, today was the best day of my life!

The best day of a twelve-year-old's life ought to be when they hit a home run in little league, get a new bike for Christmas, or take their first trip to Disney World, but instead these are students for whom the best day of their life is the one where they no longer live in fear. Murphy's philosophy: HOPE stands for 'Hold On – Possibilities Exist.' Murphy has quite possibly saved dozens, if not hundreds of lives with his presentations and follow-up programs. It is hard *not* to get involved when you are talking about kids' lives.

***

If you don't get the opportunity to attend a Sweethearts and Heroes in-person school or corporate event and you are in Vermont's northwestern corner, there's a chance that you could meet Murphy at his restaurant.

Make eye contact with Murphy, and you will not escape a significant yet awkward face-to-face engagement. It's like a solar eclipse; as if the sun is coming in, and he is casting a shadow over you, though not in a *dark* way. What you will get is an immediate and *very* direct, "Hello."

Now his attention is zeroed in on you. He is observing every component of the communication: the visual, the auditory, and the physical. Then comes the firm handshake (did I mention that Murphy's hands are like catcher's mitts?), promptly followed by, "How are you?" You robotically answer, "Good 'n' you?" Murphy replies with an endearing, slightly goofy grin, "I'm AMAZING!" Then what generally follows is an awkward conversation.

In my opinion, Murphy has an expert understanding of the human brain. That's a clumsy way to say it; I should probably describe him as a *psychology behavioral expert* or something. Simply put, he understands how the brain operates, and why people do the things they do. When Murphy engages in a sit-down conversation with you, you'll see his passion for all things intellectual. You may mention some quirk or interesting tidbit about your life, and that prompts Murphy to suggest why you may be thinking or feeling a certain way, or engaging in a specific behavior. He'll mention a recent book he's read on that particular behavior or cite one of his all-time favorite anecdotes with the inevitable punch line. It's like sitting down with a professor, coach, and shrink all in one. But it's got a contemporary feel to it. Like rock music with a violin. I speculate Murphy wants you to leave the conversation doing two things: remembering the exchange and reflecting on his mini-lesson in behavior. This has been my experience, after every conversation, without exception.

The last thing I'll mention is a line Murphy uses, and it's one of my favorites. He generally says it during your first meeting with him, early on. It doesn't matter who you are. I've arranged dozens of introductions with Murphy; from high schoolers interviewing for jobs to high-powered attorneys wishing to discuss complex business deals. It doesn't matter – Murphy is looking for insight from you, so with a touch of arrogance, he'll get in your face and ask, "What's your story?"

This always catches people off-guard, and how quickly you recover tells him a lot about you. You're being evaluated. Some people balk and say, "I dunno," and others share their life's story. Tom's gift for active listening allows him to form a relationship with you instantly. It's truly amazing to watch, and I wish I had known what was coming the first time he delivered that line to me.

Back to meeting Murphy: every time I asked him, "How are you?" he was amazing! And not just *amazing*, but AMAZING, with that ear-to-ear grin. By the way, the goofy smile doesn't match the intimidating physical appearance, but maybe that's Murphy's way of making you feel comfortable. After dozens of encounters with "amazing" replies, I felt he was onto something. New. Curious. Intellectually confounding. He was drinking the Amazing Juice, and I wanted some of that! I wondered if I could pull off amazing, without appearing to be a copycat, and achieve the same effect on the folks I meet. I decided to give it a shot!

CHAPTER TWO

First Encounters

Over the next few weeks of engaging with my fellow humans, at each interaction, I imagined what would happen if I had responded Tom Murphy style. How difficult could it be? After several days of careful consideration, I was finally ready—or so I thought—to break ground with an *amazing* reply.

I purposely selected the local coffee shop, whose staff is composed of the friendliest and least intimidating people that I see regularly. The risk was minimal. They know me. They like me! So one morning I drove to the coffee shop and went inside; just like clockwork, they greeted me. "Hi, Jay, how are you?"

I immediately reverted to autopilot and answered, "Good, 'n' you?" I had chickened out. I got my coffee and retreated to my car, defeated. I reflected on the interaction and analyzed where I had gone wrong. It was the simplest thing to execute, with the most accepting and nonjudgmental people I know; yet I froze when it was my turn at bat.

I practiced the scenario in my head a hundred times. The following morning, I drove straight to the same coffee shop to execute my plan. I walked to the counter with the intention of answering the most frequently asked question on Earth in a much more positive and upbeat manner. But again, I choked during the moment of truth. I retreated to the safety and privacy of my car once more, and firmly berated myself.

On the third day, I was sure I would not fail. But with the moment of truth looming, another customer—a stranger—suddenly appeared beside me, and I panicked. I took the path of least resistance and answered, "Good, and you?" I failed at my third attempt in a row.

What the heck was I afraid of? Me? I fly planes, requiring me to talk to Air Traffic Controllers; I'm a former alpine ski racer who has been clocked skiing downhill at over 75 MPH; I'm a former competitive triathlete. I cycled from San Diego, California, to El Paso, Texas in eight days just for fun. I've done numerous things in my life that others might consider risky. Crazy, even! But there I stood, terrified of answering a repetitive question with something more meaningful than "good."

On day four, I went to the coffee shop, hell-bent for leather. There I stood, in front of the young, smiling clerk, who seemed genuinely happy to see me. "Hi, Jay, how are you?"

I answered like a kid going through puberty. In a squeaky voice that I barely recognized, I said, "Amazing?" but it sounded more like a question than the answer I had intended to wow her with.

The clerk smiled in response and said, "Oh, amazing, huh?" Then she laughed, and I was not sure if it was my answer of "amazing" that she found humorous, or the fact that my voice had squeaked.

I got my coffee and immediately left the shop. I sat in my car; my heart was racing, my face was flush. I had done it! A shallow victory, but a victory nonetheless! There I sat, a grown man, congratulating myself for saying one word. One simple word! I had just experienced vulnerability. It reminded me of the first time I said "I love you" to a girlfriend. Maybe it was because at that time I *was* twelve and I *was* going through puberty!

But wait. I am fifty years old, and there I was celebrating my courage to say a simple word. One. Single. Word. Pathetic, right? But the feeling was real. What was going on here? I felt extremely vulnerable.

The next day I entered the coffee shop and the word *amazing* slid out a little easier. Again, the clerk found my answer funny, and she smiled. I had brightened her day. Still nervous, I left the shop and headed to work. Each subsequent day, "Amazing" rolled off the tongue a little bit easier.

After a consecutive week of this, the shop owner found herself in the mix. My action positively and powerfully influenced the staff. With friendly curiosity, she asked, "What is it with you coming in here being 'amazing' every day?" I explained that I get to pick my mood every morning. "You pick your mood?" she asked.

"Yes!" I answered. I said that I had a box of mood cards (which actually were yet to be developed) that I select from every morning. She looked at me as if I had a screw loose. But I challenged her: "If you get to choose your mood, why not pick an *amazing* one?"

iMOODivate Was Born

"What card did you pick today, Jay?" said the clerk at the coffee shop, eagerly awaiting my selection.

I had been "amazing" for two solids months. It was then that I finally got around to designing a pack of twelve cards, with the top twelve answers to the most asked question. When I received the printed cards, I headed straight to the coffee shop. I gave the first two cards to the folks working that morning. They laughed and placed them on the cash register to look at during the day.

It was then that I realized I had become a disrupter. Just like Amazon—okay, maybe that's a stretch, but in similar fashion—I had disrupted perhaps the most common, robotic verbal exchange in human communication.

I then set out to change the world! Well, at least I set out to leave my mark on it . . . in the cobwebs of my mind, I wondered how big this might become.

If you are going to try to make an impact, why not focus on people's happiness and positivity? I took an oath to myself that, when asked how I was doing, I would always reply with one of the top twelve words printed on my trigger cards. I started with close friends and upbeat strangers. Low-risk people. Results were good. Everyone seemed to like it. Sometimes I would secretly place an iMOODivate card on a friend's windshield at the gym or tuck one into the driver's side window of an acquaintance's vehicle so they'd not miss it. Within the hour, I'd receive a text or Facebook message to the effect of, "How did you know I was feeling down and needed a boost?" They expressed sincere gratitude, and meaningful connections were formed.

It dawned on me that in these very busy times, when our attention is more divided than ever, people need to know that you actually give a shit about them. With more platforms to communicate than ever before, it seems like loneliness and uncertainty are on the rise. Even if you simply notice someone for a brief moment, that is a moment in which you show you care. They suddenly no longer feel empty or alone. I became good at introducing these iMOODivate cards to many people I met.

CHAPTER THREE

Energy (My Superpower)

I recall, in my late teens, reading about the power of the brain and how the smartest person in the world was using less than 10 percent of their brain's capabilities.[2] This is a myth that has since been disproven. In fact, 90 percent of the human brain performs thousands of functions necessary to sustain our very existence, and performs them well.

Still, I was curious about the concept of untapped brain power. Thus began my life-long interest in and curiosity of the brain and its functions. This was probably not a bad thing, as I was a C student for the first three years of high school. Approaching my senior year, reality was fast approaching, and I decided it was time to start making an effort. It was time to grow up and acquire some skills with which

---

[2] Frontiers in Human Neuroscience, 08/05/2009: (Herculano-Houzel, 2002).

to support myself. Making up for lost time in education simply meant I had to put in much more time and effort. I adapted a new goal-orientated mindset. Having to play catch-up, I wondered if I could speed up my thinking and comprehension.

I wondered to myself if there was a way to increase the 10 percent of productive thought. What improvements could be made with an increase of even 1 percent?

I became intrigued by the mind and the concept of motivation as a working partnership. As a teen, I would listen to Zig Ziglar on cassette tape as I tooled around rural Vermont in my Toyota pickup truck.[3] I was young—full of what seemed like endless energy—so what was it about Zig that captivated me? Listening to him made me feel good. His teachings uplifted me, made me feel like I had a future. His message was all about individual potential. He told the most amazing stories about positivity. I listened to him every time I was alone in the car.

I dabbled in meditation, hoping to further my intellectual development. Unfortunately, that didn't stick. In the '80s it seemed like the only people who were meditating were ones who were into alternative lifestyles and UFOs. Today, meditation is not only a widely accepted strategy for improved mindfulness for us common folk, but it's also become an essen-

---

[3] www.washingtonpost.com/local/obituaries/zig-ziglar-upbeat-motivational-speaker-and-author-dies-at-86/2012/11/28/b52bd4ea-397e-11e2-8a97-363b0f9a0ab3_story.html

tial skill adopted by many successful people. There's a long list of athletes, celebrities, and industry leaders who have developed a routine for mindfulness, where meditation is a staple.

In my experience, when you completely immerse yourself in something, as I had in Zig Ziglar's philosophy, it is far easier for the message to impact you, to live inside and take root. And that is truly my hope for you as you read this book—that you will find meaning in it, in one of its chapters, or even in just a couple of paragraphs, and that it will stick. I feel certain that it has the potential to impact your life in a very positive way, in a way that you might not yet understand. I hope you will commit to the program, make yourself vulnerable, and take an amazing leap of faith. How?

Say. One. Word.

It is my belief that there *is* excess brain power to tap into, but we are not yet consciously ready to do so. Or perhaps it simply requires a different method of thinking or processing information. How many times have you concluded something subconsciously without slow, careful thought? It just came to you. I am a believer in energy, that there are energy waves transmitting from your mind all the time, and I feel that others have the same potential—though often untapped—to receive them.

Before I continue, how many times has your gut told you something was so and it turned out to be right? How many times have you had a hunch that proved true? Ever had a vision of an episode only to have it happen moments later? My belief is that your subconscious accepted some energy signal. The message was delivered; you just didn't know how to process it in your *conscious* mind.

Perhaps it is all just a simple battle of speed. Your brain could theoretically (no one really knows) process eleven million bits of information, yet experts say you can't exceed sixty bits per second [4]. Which poses the question: what happens to the bits of information that we are unable to process, and how does your brain decide which bits of information to process and which bits to ignore? Are those unprocessed bits of information then discarded, or do they go somewhere for further evaluation? My mind hurts just thinking about it! But taking it a step further - what if we had the power to increase the speed from 60 bps? Might it be possible to increase these processing speeds over time by natural progression? Will people in the year 2200 be processing at 100 bps? And lastly, is there some sort of method of processing this additional information using a technique other than conscious thought?

Let's look to the younger generation for a moment. Facebook is for old folks, who "ruined" it for them. Then we migrated to Instagram and inadvertently drove many kids away from it to their current and favorite application, Snapchat. I have an eighteen-year-old daughter, who, like many kids, is

---

[4] https://www.technologyreview.com/2009/08/25/210267/new-measure-of-human-brain-processing-speed/

practically addicted to her phone. When she communicates with her friends, frequently spoken or written words are not used – the communication is in pictures. I will watch her crank off twenty separate snaps to twenty different friends, each obtaining a different selfie of her. She apparently customized each look to represent some sort of unique kid-to-kid message. Head tilted one way for one friend, the other for someone else. Head up, then head down. Left side, right side. A seemingly endless library of poses per snap request. My point is that the human brain, in my opinion, was not originally engineered for word processing; it was engineered for picture processing. It has been said that a picture is worth a thousand words, and maybe, much to my frustration, a new form of speedier communication is taking place. And it pains me to acknowledge the good in this, but as a scientific-style thinker, I must go with the science, or at the very least examine the hypothesis to one conclusion or another. What if this is an intermediate step toward faster information processing? Are we in the middle of a mental processing speed upgrade?

If this truly demonstrates a new, higher-speed gear than speaking and reading achieves, what is the next step? Might it be some combination of information transition from pictures to radio waves or this thing called 'energy?' Allow me to offer some personal examples where energy was used to solve problems:

I was a computer programming major in college. On one occasion, I was coding some homework using the programming language COBOL. For those not familiar with COBOL, it was a major computer language that was widely popular; in the '70s, '80s, and '90s, many computer mainframes ran COBOL. It was embraced by banks and other financial institutions in particular. In those days, if you were in college to become a computer programmer, gaining mastery of COBOL was mandatory. Like many computer programming languages, if just one character is out of place, the entire program could completely fail. I was about to embark on my fourth day of trying to debug a program I had written from scratch. It was frustrating. I reread each line over and over again trying to find the bug – like looking for a needle in a haystack. It was similar to a word jumble, where you seek the first letter of a word, but when you find it, the rest of the letters around it aren't correct. After an entire evening of this, I gave up and hoped for clarity in the morning after a good night's sleep.

    I recall very early the next morning, the sun was just barely rising, and I was still asleep in my room. My eyes were closed, yet I could see everything in the room vividly. The windows over my bed were cracked open, and a slight breeze blew the curtains. I could see it all. I was *asleep*, but in some zone.

    My mind slowly wandered to the computer program, and I saw, in my mind's eye, the green bar computer paper. It's called *green bar paper*, as back then, when you printed out your program on paper to look at, it alternated horizontally between roughly one-inch bars of a light mint green and then subsequent natural paper color. Hence the name *green bar*.

My mind scanned the program code line by line, like watching a typewriter in action. I stopped halfway down on the third page, where the line containing the error was almost magically highlighted, and the typo was presented to me as a reversed or negative image, to draw my attention to the mistake. It was a flashing beacon. When I woke up, I went directly to my desk and pulled out the green bar. I flipped to the page in question that my "dream" showed me, and there was the bug, exactly as I had seen it in my mind's eye. BOOM! I was stunned.

After that, I slept with the green bar and a pen beside my bed. The computer green bar phenomenon happened three or four times during my computer programming career, which was not only super helpful, but also opened my eyes to this "superpower." The other 90 percent of my brain was doing *something*, and for a brief moment I had tapped into its magic.

I would caution you not to try to force yourself into this trance. In fact, I find the more you force it, the faster it will escape you. It's not something that I can turn on when I want to. However, I've found that—in my case—water seems to enhance this superpower. Over the years my best and most insightful epiphanies came to me in or near water. For me, washing dishes and showering are among the top activities to induce amazing insight and those "eureka" moments. I have come to believe that mindless activity allows your subconscious to relax and be open to receiving energy, a meditation of sorts. I'm training my brain to relax, clear the clutter, and find the meaning or purpose in the top matters of the current time.

Great ideas are not the only attributes that occur during this hypnotic state. I find that when interacting with people, I more easily pick up on nonverbal communication, most of which I suspect is received subconsciously. I think it happens so fast that I simply cannot process it consciously. There are hundreds of ways that the eyes, nose, forehead, mouth, jaw, and overall head gestures communicate information. Within this one-on-one communication, you can pick up on hidden truths.

Consider communication in terms of spoken language. English can be a difficult language to be socially proficient at, for example. It is complex because one word can have many different meanings, which can easily confuse a listener. When someone is talking to me, I am working hard to understand—what do they really want or really mean, what are they really *saying*? Part of what I'm doing is comprehending the words they've chosen—or even more importantly the words they *avoided*—that might help me get to the crux of their statement. A simple and worn-out example of this is when someone says, "It's not about the money." That sentence is a sure signal that it is, in fact, about the money. Or when ending a relationship, one party says, "It's not you, it's *me*."

After over forty plus years of pondering what the mind is doing and why it is doing it, and having read many books and articles on how the mind operates and human behavior, I have concluded that this is *my* superpower, and it is centered on energy. If we are both in the right frame of mind, I can send energy, and the intended recipient can receive it. This should not be confused with mind reading; it is *sensing energy*. Sometimes I cannot determine initially if it is good energy or bad; I can only tell that there is much activity going on and information that needs to change hands—or should I say *minds*.

Through years of practicing *super observations*, as I call them, I have found that I frequently experience information overload. If I'm in a group of ten or so people and everyone is talking, I can't handle all of the communication coming at me, and I find it difficult to focus. Often, I have become exhausted quickly and have had to leave a party or step away to refocus. This is an issue with hypersensitivity—processing the sheer volume of information coming your way. I just can't process it all and become overloaded.

Overall, however, it's a pretty cool superpower to have! It comes and goes, and I have not yet learned to control it, but I'm more than thrilled when it does present itself. It's a gift. Having this hypersensitivity allows me to pick up signals from people and leaves me to decide whether to engage in conversation or to leave them be—*or* to hand them a card. I don't always get it right, but the lesson here is that **the entire program is about the willingness to heighten your sense of awareness**. It is the same with your moods, being aware that you do indeed have a choice, an awareness, and the ability to nudge the needle to the better, just a touch. In a fraction of a second, you can truly impact peoples' lives, by simply putting some positive energy into the universe. I submit that when you try the iMOODivate program just one fraction of a second at a time and answer the world's most common question with what is printed on your trigger card, your mood will drastically improve. Whether you need it or not. And let's be honest – nearly *all* of us need it.

Okay: let's think big for a moment. Imagine the sheer power of one billion people trying to be slightly more positive, slightly happier for just a moment. Imagine the power of this unnamed energy source filled with positivity. And imagine all the people that might be sensitive to this energy but don't know it yet; how it would boost their mood and, with an improved frame of mind, send *their* happiness out into the universe for others. It might sound crazy, but I have experienced way too many successes in my life for this to be coincidental.

Even if I am not 100 percent right, I guarantee that I'm not 100 percent wrong. Take even a 1 percent correction and multiply that by a billion people. *Then* tell me it doesn't make a difference. That's math I can get behind.

CHAPTER FOUR

Dave

Several months after I began connecting with locals and feeling the thrill of iMOODivating people, an acquaintance came to my office to discuss business. The guy was a full-bearded, lean, mean, wrecking machine. If you met him in public, you would keep an eye on him, as he looked the type that could snap at any moment. As a matter of fact, Dave *had* done time—twice. Low-level offenses, I think; the result of a barroom brawl, maybe a traffic incident or something of that nature. He gave the impression that he was fearless. His look and attitude were unique.

I first met Dave years ago when he was working at a local lumberyard. I walked into the yard wearing a shirt that had MUSKOKA printed on the front. Muskoka is a lakes region of Ontario, and I had never met anyone in Northwestern Vermont with ties to the place. That is, until I met Dave, who immediately responded to the shirt, "Hey, I'm from there!"

After that, whenever I visited the lumberyard, Dave would call me "Muskoka." That was our connection. Despite this rapport, a guy like Dave would be the last person I would approach to iMOODivate. Or so I thought.

Dave did *not* seem the type to be influenced by the warm and fuzzy "have a nice day" kind of stuff. But one day I just got a feeling or vision; I stuck my neck out and left a card on his Harley when he was in the gym, about three months prior to our office meeting.

Until then, I had only given cards to people that I considered nonthreatening and accepting. People I knew well and could be vulnerable with. But that day I acted on a hunch: at the gym, I paid attention to Dave's nonverbal cues. On this day he was signaling that something was going on inside. He didn't make eye contact with me; his brow was furrowed. My superpower kicked into full gear, and I sensed that he had a lot going on. Sometimes it happens so fast that it can be hard to comprehend the message coming at me. But on that day, Dave needed *something*.

Back to our office meeting, halfway through the conversation, Dave spotted a single iMOODivate card on my desk. He stopped mid-sentence. "Where'd you get that card?" he bellowed sternly, the finger at the end of his outstretched arm pointing toward the card. I confessed that I had been giving the cards out for the last few months here and there. He interrupted, "You left one on my Harley three months ago at the gym!" By his tone, I thought he might be angry. Had I scratched the paint? I waited for him to continue. Dave attempted a smile. "I put it on my fridge, and I read it every day before I go out the door to work. It changed my life!" He smiled broadly now, exposing one chipped front tooth. Dave's attitude took me by surprise. It was not Dave's usual style!

Later, I wondered how my little card could have made a tough man melt. How much power did these cards hold? I honed my pitch to: "I am building an army of positivity to combat negativity." What I found was that deep down, most everyone wants to be happy—or at least happier. Onward I marched.

CHAPTER FIVE

Allison

I had made the acquaintance of a woman who taught first grade at a local public school, Allison. We had met at an early morning spin class.

Spin class, especially of the early morning variety, does not foster a lot of conversation or small talk. Folks enter and give the monotonous and unsolicited, "Morning," as they shuffle along to their designated bikes. They set up and warm up quietly, then wait for the class to begin.

In this environment, I found it easy to assess others' mental states—knowingly or unknowingly—by simply observing them and their body language. I call it *energy observation*, and on this particular morning, I was in high gear. I observed Allison and sensed a deep disturbance.

She did, indeed, have lots on her mind. Allison had been through a difficult divorce and subsequent relationships that hadn't gone well. Anyone might have guessed that her mind would be busy. She covered it well, smiled a lot, but I sensed that something was weighing heavily on her that day. The smile seemed forced, her eyes darted back down low in front of her, things like that.

Our friendship was new: we were on a first-name basis and occasionally after class exchanged polite chit-chat, but nothing more. I did not yet know the history of her personal life, but I sensed that her mind was busy. I had not handed out very many cards, and I was far from being brave enough to get in her face Tom Murphy style. So, I adopted a softer, more passive approach. As I passed her car in the parking lot, I had a vision of brightening her day, so I stuck a card under her windshield wiper. Within the hour, she did some asking around and discovered that I'd been leaving cards on cars in the gym parking lot. I received her Facebook friend request and a private message: "I was really struggling this morning with all that's going on in my life, and the card you left on my car really turned my day around. I was at a low point, and this made all the difference in the world to me. How did you know? Thank you!"

I responded that I didn't know anything about her personal life and had just sensed some energy. I had thought it would be nice to drop a note on her car. Allison loved the concept. I went through the program details with her, explaining how your attitude is the only thing over which you have full control. She asked if it would be appropriate to introduce the concept to her first-grade class. We agreed it would be an interesting experiment to see how young minds would respond. I set her up with an entire set of cards.

A few days later, Allison shared a video of the cutest thing: She had instructed her students to pick their moods and recorded their responses. Imagine six- and seven-year-olds trying to say words like *magnificent* and *phenomenal*. I think we even got something close to *stupendous* from one little superhero. The takeaway from the experiment was that the time to train the mind for a more positive approach to life is early on.

Having never been on the receiving end of an iMOODivate experience I wanted to know, from real people in the wild, what their experiences were like. I asked Allison, and here's how she responded. These are her own words, unedited, un-coached:

> *The first thing anyone reading this should know is what exactly it means to be "Imoodivated". The moment I was handed that card that read "I Choose to Feel Amazing", my first thought was "are you kidding me?". "Amazing" was a far cry from what I was feeling. I was at an ultimate low...in a very sad and dark place emotionally...completely and utterly powerless.*

But, was I? I'm pretty sure that Jay Cummings isn't a mind reader, but he could not have chosen a better moment to hand me that card and give me a brief, yet powerful explanation about what those words, printed on that card meant. A "bad" event had occurred in my life, but in that moment, I realized that I did have power. I absolutely had the power to decide how I was going to choose to feel. That moment was serendipitous.

Most times in life when someone hands you something that looks like it might be some sort of propaganda, your warning bells sound. You get that feeling that you're about to be sold something. Oftentimes it's from a friend or an acquaintance who has embarked on some new business or network marketing endeavor. So, you brace yourself for the speech...the pitch. You choose whether or not this is something that interests you and if so, at what cost.

Then there are those times when you receive a gift...purely from the heart. It might be a birth-

day gift, Christmas present or even a sympathy card. There are no strings attached. This is a gesture that tells you that this person cares about you and wants you to feel loved and/or comforted.

When someone gives you an Imoodivate card, they are giving you something entirely different. They are giving you an assignment. This assignment is a gift, with the selfish interest of the giver that if you complete the assignment, you will make your life and the lives of everyone you encounter better, including their own.

We all know that moods are contagious and we should all know that they absolutely affect our physical health. We eat healthy, take vitamins and exercise to take care of our bodies and minds. We avoid things that are unhealthy or toxic to our bodies, but do we do this for our minds?

What we say to ourselves each day when our feet hit the floor is just as vital to our health as anything else. When you tell yourself how tired you are, how stressed out you are, how depressed or unmotivated you are, even how angry or frustrated you might be, you carry those emotions with you throughout your day and they impact every single encounter you have.

Just a few days ago, I woke up and told myself that today, I was going to choose to feel amazing. I also decided to follow Mr. Marlow's 5 before 9:00 rule. The goal of this rule is to make 5 positive contacts before 9:00 am. Not only does this rule impact the 5 people you encounter and interact with, but it impacts you because it forces you to seek out and create positive energy.

A colleague of mine was in my classroom giving an SBAC overview to my Fourth Grade class. I found myself staring at her in absolute awe of how much weight she has lost in the past year. I didn't get a chance to tell her that day as she was teaching in front of my class, but the next morning she made the 5 before 9:00 list.

I told her how amazing she looked. I also asked her how she did it. She beamed as she answered my question. She explained that it was just small changes over time. There were no programs or shakes or magic pills.

She just made small changes in her diet that lead to an increase in her metabolism and probably some stomach shrinkage allowing her to crave less food.

There are two lessons in this short story. Mine and hers. Mine was the power of a positive observation about another human being, leading to a compliment, causing a shift in their mood. Hers was that small changes over time lead to incredible results.

Imagine combining those two lessons. Create a small change in your life everyday and then spread positivity.

So, each day I tell myself how I am going to feel. Then, I spread it. My mood changes and the moods of others around me change.

The morning after spin class when Jay Imoodivated me changed my life. I had every reason to feel hurt and angry. What was going on for me that day doesn't really matter. What matters is that I took back my power and chose how I was going to feel regardless of what had happened.

I find that Imoodivating myself; choosing how I'm going to feel each and every day has a huge impact on myself and those around me. At first it feels completely awkward. The first time someone asked "Hey Allison, how are you?" and I responded "Amazing" it didn't feel natural. After a few months, and now years, it felt and feels more than comfortable. In fact, I can't imagine saying "good" now. I shudder at the "not bad", "alright" or "OK" responses. When those responses come out of my mouth now (which they occasionally still do), I'm disappointed and correct myself.

Who wants to feel not bad, alright or OK? I want the people in my life to feel more than that. Those moods are mundane. I don't want anyone around me to feel mundane. If my children feel simply not bad, I feel like they have a mood fever. A mood fever is just like a body fever. It means something isn't well. When something isn't well with your body, you might take a sick day and do what you need to do to fix it: rest, medicine, etc.

I do the same with my mood now. Living through a pandemic is certainly a challenge to one's mental health. When I found myself waking up feeling less than great, I rejoined the gym, started making better dietary choices and even had some counseling sessions. In little time, I was able to wake up and say amazing again.

If you wake up physically healthy with all of your basic needs met, you should feel incredible, amazing, magnificent, fabulous. Anything less is for those who don't.

CHAPTER SIX

Dan

I first met Dan Marlow in the spring of my fifth-grade year at school. He was the new athletic director of the local elementary/middle school.

Dan went from classroom to classroom introducing himself as the phys ed teacher for the following school year and announcing that, as such, he planned to start a soccer program (soccer was new to Vermont). Dan exhibited positive energy; it was evident in his smile and in his delivery. In that second, I decided I would try out for soccer in the fall. Not because Dan had sold me on the idea of playing soccer, but because of the way he made me feel. I talked to my friends about Mr. Marlow, soccer, and the excitement of the upcoming season. Most were moved - I was inspired!

The following fall, I was among the first to sign up for soccer. I vividly recall that the season was hotter than the calendar indicated. We trained and sprinted to build physical conditioning. I was a sixth grader who would have ordinarily been intimidated by playing with seventh and eighth graders, a couple of whom were sporting beards! But I didn't care. Dan inspired me to play the first time I heard him speak. One of the attributes of an excellent motivator is that you feel they are speaking to you alone, and such was the case with Dan. I did not know anything about soccer, but I trusted that Dan would help me learn. He was demanding and tough, but he fostered an environment that made you want to excel. And when you fell short, Dan motivated you to keep trying. He never gave up on you, which only cemented your belief in yourself.

Dan later moved on to the local high school, where he remains athletic director today. He had a long career coaching the high school soccer program, where he continued to exercise his gift to motivate. *No* was not a word you would find in Dan's vocabulary. Instead, it was, "Yes, you can," "We'll try," "We'll figure it out." Failure was never an option, and even if you did not succeed to the degree you wanted, he always emphasized the positive.

For over fifty years, Mr. Marlow motivated and supported students in all things athletic - and more. This produced a ripple effect, reaching into students' personal and academic lives. Dan became known as the Master Motivator; some said he could motivate a rock to move from one side of the room to the other. His positivity and motivation were unwavering. It was as if we had our very own Tony Robbins right in our backyard.

For me, it was a natural transition—listening to Dan Marlow during the school day and to Zig Ziglar during the summer and on weekends. What I did not realize is that I was being conditioned. All I knew was that it felt good to feel good.

In the previous chapter, I mentioned attending a spin class at the local gym. What I didn't mention is that Dan Marlow was the instructor! For the last twenty years, Dan - on top of all his other personal and professional commitments - would be up and raring to go at 5:00 a.m. to lead spin classes. There, Dan provides encouragement via commentary. "Half of the county just hit the 'lose' button on their alarm clocks! They'll never catch up with you today!" "Be who you say you are." And many, many more bits of inspiration.

You see, Dan immerses himself in positivity. He reads all the motivational material he can get his hands on. While he has his own positive messages, he's happy to share others'. Picture this: You are pedaling your butt off in a spin class, sweat dripping down your face, neck, and back. Heat is radiating from your head. Your breath is coming fast and hard. Then Dan pulls out this quote from motivational speaker Les Brown at the perfect time:

> Imagine if you will, being on your deathbed. And standing around your bed are the ghosts of

the ideas, the dreams, the abilities, the talents given to you by life. And that you—for whatever reason—you never acted on those ideas, you never pursued that dream, you never used those talents, we never saw your leadership, you never used your voice, you never wrote that book.

And there they are standing around your bed looking at you with large, angry eyes, saying, "We came to you, and only you could have given us life! Now we must die with you forever."

The question is: If you die today, what ideas, what dreams, what abilities, what talents, what gifts, would die with you?

Moments earlier you felt that you had reached your max, and you could not push on any further. Then you hear that little gem, and suddenly, you have a gear you never knew you had. Somehow you find the wherewithal to dig down deeper and pusher harder than you have ever pushed before. It was no coincidence that I started writing this book the same day I first heard that nugget.

The point is it's your mindset, your *attitude* that sets artificial boundaries, and Dan knows how and when to break through them. He can motivate you to go further than you ever thought you could go. He knows, from fifty years of coaching students, what to look for; on your face, in your eyes. He motivates you to achieve what - just moments earlier, you thought was impossible. And the iMOODivate program is similar to that, inspiring you to do something you previously thought was impossible. Both methods produce the same outcome, achieving something you originally thought was unattainable.

CHAPTER SEVEN

Tribute: Loren Poirier

The Poirier kids grew up just down the road from my two older brothers and me. Their father, Donald, was one of the most positive people I have ever met. Even from an early age, I remember Donald as a chipper man. If he was ever angry or down in the dumps, he did not show it, and I never saw it!

Donald and his wife had six children, whose names all began with the letter *L*. As a kid, I thought that was a little geeky. It was their trademark, however, and people who knew them embraced it. I have known the Poirier family for more than fifty years, and I can honestly tell you I have never heard one of them swear. Gentle, polite, gosh, shucks, country-style family folks. I did not have that level of discipline, and I still don't, but I was always impressed by their happiness and their kindness. Theirs was an example to follow.

The first disaster to strike the family was when one of their young adult daughters died of complications following childbirth. I couldn't imagine the range of emotions the Poirier's were experiencing—to go from the jubilation of welcoming a new grandchild to the tragic and unexpected loss of their daughter.

Years later, after Donald's retirement, his wife was diagnosed with cancer, which she battled until her death a few years later. Funerals were something I tried to avoid, but this was one I had to attend; the Poirier's meant that much to me. When I spoke with Donald at the wake, he was obviously saddened; though, if crushed, he hid it well. I awkwardly offered condolences, and Donald, sensing my unease throughout the encounter, simply said, "What are you going to do?" and shrugged his shoulders. I reflected upon this interaction, and perhaps Donald, sensing my discomfort, was in fact consoling *me*. He was good at comforting others, even during his time of need.

Throughout his adulthood, Donald suffered several serious medical issues but always recovered. Some of the issues were heart-related. I believe it was Donald's positivity that carried him through.

***

A few years ago, I reached a crossroads. iMOO-Divate was not going anywhere: I hadn't done a video or sold a card in months. It seemed to be dying a slow death. I questioned why I had even started such a movement. A couple of acquaintances mocked it (it is easy to find fault when you have nothing else to offer). I kept filing tax returns with minimal revenue and heavy losses, and it reached the point where my CPA began asking, "Why are you doing this?" I could not verbalize a great answer other than, "I feel next year will be the year it catches on."

One day during this low point, as I was leaving the grocery store, I saw Loren Poirier. He was a few years older than I, and we had always exchanged pleasantries when we met, then continued on our way. It was a dark time for me personally, and for iMOODivate. When I saw Loren, I was tempted to keep my head down, forego the usual chit-chat and just get home, but our eyes met, and I felt compelled to at least say hello. As in the book *Celestine Prophecies*, there are no coincidences. We had information to exchange at this seemingly random meeting, and it did not happen by accident.

Loren said, "Jay, I have to tell you how much I enjoy the iMOODivate program. I really love it—it resonates with me." That was all I needed to hear! I perked right up and dove into conversation with Loren. He told me how the program had impacted his life. I produced a handful of cards (which I always carried with me) and asked him to select one. He seemed grateful, and appreciative of the gift. I thanked him for taking the time to chat and confessed that I had been on the verge of giving up on iMOODivate. He strongly recommended that I keep going. And I did, solely thanks to Loren.

The following summer, tragedy struck the Poirier family again. Loren was killed in a freak motorcycle accident. He had been a tremendous person, a by-the-book kind of guy. I doubt his truck or motorcycle *ever* exceeded the speed limit. That was the way he lived his life. When I heard about the accident, I knew he could not have been at fault. He wasn't. Another vehicle drifted over the centerline and hit him head on.

I immediately felt deep, personal sorrow and pain for the family for having to endure yet another tragedy. They say God never gives you more than you can handle, but I cannot imagine having to experience even one of these events, let alone three deaths of immediate family members. Loren's funeral was very well attended, and this third tragedy seemed to have taken its toll on Donald. In time, Donald eventually returned to a positive mindset, but it is hard to comprehend how, considering the pain he must have carried within.

Loren's younger brother, Lyle, is my friend and coworker. I wanted to reach out to him but waited until he'd had some time to grieve. Ironically, Lyle used this time to prepare something for me.

When we later connected, I told Lyle how his brother single-handedly saved iMOODivate. Loren sensed something in me, and *he* took the opportunity to iMOODivate *me*! He'd spotted me at one of my low points and delivered a message that saved the program. As I shared this memory with Lyle, I had a tear in my eye, yet Lyle had a slight smile on his face. His reaction did not align with the situation, or so I thought.

Lyle dug into his pocket and pulled out the iMOODivate card I had given to Loren that day at the grocery store. He said his brother loved the concept and spoke about it often to family and friends—and especially to Lyle. I had had no idea that upbeat, positive-minded Loren not only had needed but also *used* the program. Yet Lyle revealed that Loren kept the card neatly tucked into his laptop and referred to it often. My tears welled up even further. I felt compelled to give Lyle a hug; I think I needed it more than he did.

This chapter is a tribute to the entire Poirier family, and especially to Loren. Loren, if it weren't for you reaching out, taking a chance, and letting me know how you enjoyed the videos and the posts on Facebook, iMOODivate would have been buried with you. Ride on, brother. Ride on.

CHAPTER EIGHT

Mitch Durfee

I met Mitch's company before I met Mitch.

Mitch is more than twenty years my junior – you would think that a 20-something skateboarder would have little in common with an old guy like me. A hipster I am not! But we both shared the attribute of focused entrepreneurialism. Our destiny was not only to meet, but to collaborate and establish an enduring friendship.

Let me back up a little bit. I started a business many years ago (which I'll describe in a subsequent chapter), and I sold it when it no longer suited me. After I sold my business, I wanted to take a year off and clear my head. Twenty-one years of running a production facility will grind on you. As any entrepreneur will tell you, when you own a business, you are never off the clock. My wife predicted that my break wouldn't last a week. Yet I made it to the end of week two—so there! I was recruited by and accepted a job at a local community bank as their business development representative. I was hired as the non-banker banker to give a different perspective. I soon convinced the top brass to let me offer no-fee business consulting to help businesses grow or improve. The idea was that takers might appreciate the effort and become customers of the bank. It worked! Who wouldn't want a business consultant helping them grow their business, at no cost to them? And one with decades of local experience, no less?

My job was to network with businesses in the area and "make rain." I kept seeing one business around town: Grunts Move Junk. It had all the makings of a national brand; in fact, I thought it *was* a local franchise of a national brand. It was brilliantly branded and seemed to be everywhere. And I—the guy who knows *everyone*—did not know who was running this outfit. To find out, I simply called the 800 number and asked, "Who are you?"

I arranged a meeting with the owner of Grunts Move Junk, Mitch Durfee. Coincidentally, I knew his dad, his uncle, and his grandfather—in fact, his granddad had been one of my teachers in junior high school. Mitch entered the bank and seemed a little distracted. His answers to my initial questions were short. He was trying to figure out my angle.

I dove into some of his marketing, and he was coy, possibly suspicious that I was working an angle for a competitor. When I confessed my misinterpretation of his business as a franchise of a national brand and complimented him on the presence of the brand, he let his guard down. The business was his and only his, and he had just one location at the time. Mitch was doing everything right. And simply put, like me, Mitch had been able to create something out of nothing.

Grunts Move Junk was an organization he created to employ military veterans. Mitch had just gotten out of the army, and it was clear that he was not your average hourly wage earner. His business concept was brilliant. The pro-veteran sentiment in the country was at an all-time high after lengthy deployments in Iraq. It was 2014, and there were hundreds of veterans returning from one, two, three, even four deployments, now stateside and looking for work.

What do the Grunts do? They hop into a truck, pick up heavy stuff and bring it somewhere. Customers trust veterans, who perform their services with military precision. Mitch billed out his crew at $55 an hour per "grunt", with a minimum of two hours per pair of grunts. Often, crews could get to customers' homes the same day the request was received.

People tend to have a lot of crap they want hauled off to the dump. In addition, they might ask to have their lawn mown, leaves raked, furniture moved, or appliances delivered. You name it, people paid $55 an hour for it. This shocked me, as the going rate to hire a landscaper was about $25 an hour. Folks gladly paid $55 for a veteran's services, especially with such a quick response.

IMOODIVATE

The business's services expanded to include construction, which came as somewhat of a surprise to me. At the time, a highly qualified, skilled craftsman was getting $35-$40 an hour for their services, but folks hired Grunts at their more expensive rate and kept them busy all day long. The veterans had untapped skills and quickly figured out how to accommodate the requests. They started with roofing jobs and bathroom remodels, and by the time Mitch sold the company, they were doing residential and commercial demos and remodeling.

Grunts' success could be attributed to its accessibility: answering the phone, saying yes, and actually showing up. Many of the trades in Vermont were so busy they either never returned phone calls or kept putting the job off for days, weeks, or even months. When a Grunt shows up in twenty-four hours, that's a game changer! It was a triumph, and even though he had expanded his business to three locations—and I predicted he was destined to grow to as many as two hundred franchises—Mitch was bored. He had set his sights on bigger goals. Soon after establishing a franchise in Phoenix, Arizona, he was lured into attending a Tony Robbins event in the same city.[5]

I got a text from Mitch saying that he was in Phoenix, planning to attend a Tony Robbins Business Mastery Event. The cost was $10,000 for the week, and he further explained that if you didn't get 'a mil-

---

[5] Tony Robbins: www.britannica.com/biography/Tony-Robbins

lion dollars' worth of value from the seminar, you could get your money back.

The training worked. During the first month after the event, Mitch added $25K to the bottom line. He was hooked! He shared some of the cutting-edge strategies and techniques he had been introduced to. As a preferred customer of Tony Robbins, he received two tickets to Tony's UPW (Unleash the Power Within) seminar. Two months later, Mitch and I were on our way to San José, California, to attend.

We arrived at the arena at 10:00 a.m., which was packed with twelve thousand attendees. Tony took the stage at 11:00 a.m., and we were launched into the craziest three days of our lives.

A Tony Robbins UPW is a three-day, fifty-hour motivation session and rock concert all rolled into one. We became so enthralled that we had no idea how fast time was passing. Everyone in the arena yelled and screamed at the top of their lungs, pledging to total strangers their new, unwavering belief in the immediate changes they were making to better their lives. We were so excited and convinced of higher achievements in life that failure seemed impossible! The positive high you get at one of these seminars is like a mega-shot of oxytocin. I said *oxytocin*, not the other one. Oxytocin is the chemical in your brain that, well, makes you happy. Toward the end of day one, there is a two-to-three-hour long training event (it felt shorter) where attendees learn to walk on fire! During the day while we were all inside an air-conditioned arena being motivated by Tony and his crew,

Tony's staff was outside building fires. They had built roughly twenty, twenty five-foot lanes of red-hot glowing coals. The end of day one concluded with most attendees walking on hot coals. It was a giant mental achievement. You'd better believe *that* took a leap of faith! People broke through their self-limiting beliefs.

From a marketing standpoint, it was a brilliant way to have people buy into what you're selling. If there ever was a way to set a hook, that was it. The evening concluded with Mitch and me flying high. I've never felt more mentally positive! Yet I could tell that Mitch had just scratched the surface.

He had relentless energy and little fear. He was smart; taught himself how to start a business with just an idea and a book or two. He was a self-taught marketing genius; running Facebook ads, Google ads, Google analytics, email marketing campaigns, and much more. He bought investment properties and began a career in public speaking.

He could engage in a conversation with anyone, anywhere, and he was always on his *A* game. I've watched him work a room; collecting phone numbers and scheduling meetings with anyone he wanted. He sought to achieve goals of the highest standard. If you asked me to predict which friend in my inner circle would become a self-made billionaire, without question, I'd say it would be Mitch!

I returned from the UPW so positive that I was practically unbearable to those around me. Negative people were now invisible to me, and I was on the road to greatness. I had a record year at the bank, was promoted to officer and VP; Mitch sold Grunts Move Junk and his house in Vermont and moved to Florida with a pocket full of cash and a positive mentality. What would he do next? Whatever the hell he wanted!

iMOODivate was flowing everywhere Mitch and I went. I felt truly amazing and was no longer apprehensive talking about it; indeed, it naturally exuded from my persona. I was the most positive I have ever been in my life, and I make this recommendation to everyone I meet: check out at least one UPW in your lifetime. My wife and daughter did just that the following summer, and they loved it. It was all thanks to Mitch.

CHAPTER NINE

My First Nosedive in MOOD

Six months after beginning my journey down the good mood road, it happened: I crashed. I wasn't happy. My wife, Jennifer, and I had gotten into an argument about something or another. I can still recall how pissed off I was. More than twenty years of marriage had taught me that fighting back in the heat of the moment, while it might feel good, only makes matters worse in the long run. I have a theory about these kinds of situations: if you are in an argument with someone and the dialogue goes back and forth three times like a game of ping-pong, you're no longer fighting about the original topic; you're fighting about how you fight. Truths become distorted to avoid admitting fault, and you quickly point your finger at the other to achieve the moral high ground. And if you cannot make the jump to some twisted truth, you can always dig up some old grievance from twenty years prior. I used to keep an arsenal of past grievances for such occasions. But here, I chose instead to retreat to my home office, located in the detached garage. It was a Saturday morning in the dead of winter. In the sanctity of my man cave, I was certain that I was 100 percent right. However, I was equally certain that Jennifer would never admit wrongdoing. I entertained the idea that she felt 100 percent right as well.

I wasted time questioning her sincerity and her position on whatever topic it was that we argued about. Given my negative mood, I honestly would have preferred to blow something up. When I'm in that state, I typically grab the chain saw with a full tank of gas, chaps, and corks, and traipse out to the back thirty to take down a dead tree or two. One tank of gas lasts about an hour, and the physical activity makes me feel like enough of a man to then return home ready for calmer discussion. Really bad situations require two tanks of gas. But on that Saturday, I had a schedule to keep: I had to produce and release my weekly iMOODivate video. I dove into it, though my heart wasn't in the work.

I had written solid material in my head earlier that week; prime stuff. On the other hand, I was still pissed that my good mood streak had ended. I knew it would have to end sometime, yet I had fantasized about endless positivity. Now my mind revisited the argument, and I wondered for a moment if it was her fault that I was unhappy. Could she be standing in the way of my full, future potential?

I grabbed my camera and rushed to set it up. The mechanism was not locking like it should have, and the equipment tipped over, compounding my frustration, but I plowed forward. Take one! My first word and every subsequent one was horrible—empty—flat. Anyone with minimal observation skills would be able to see this, and their mood would be worsened. I mean, I was supposed to *improve* moods, not *ruin* them! Takes 2, 3, 4, 5, 6, 7, 8, 9, 10, I couldn't get it right! Not even close.

I started to question my own positivity. Was I ruined? Had I contaminated my ability to choose my mood forever? Was I a fraud? All I had to do was produce a three-minute message of positive, motivational content, but I was struggling. Badly.

I attempted several more takes and deemed the last usable, albeit barely. If I was being honest with myself, it still sucked! Not as bad as the first ten takes, though still not ready for release. But there *was* progress. I had made growth in the right direction. I decided to take a break and headed inside for breakfast.

When I entered the house, my eyes instantly locked onto Jennifer's. I gave a greeting without emotion of, "Morning," and she replied in kind. She didn't hate me, so that was a plus. Things were looking up!

After a hot breakfast, I headed back to the office and recorded five more attempts. I do not think anyone would have been able to tell where my mind was before I recorded the final take, and I was relieved that I had something I could release to the wild. I felt a whole lot better.

Historically, when my mood has taken a dive, it has taken me about a week to recover into solidly positive territory. Yet once I had sent my video out, on a mood scale of 1–10, I was at a solid six, and felt that I was trending upward. I continued that trajectory for the next two hours in what I call *forced self-therapy*. This is where I *pretend* to be happy, on camera, alone, and in the privacy of my own space. I kept thinking back to Amy Cuddy's Ted Talk: "Fake It till You Make It."[6] There, alone in that little corner of my garage, I bypassed seven days of doom and gloom in just two hours. I faked it till I made it. Thank you, Ms. Cuddy!

But let's examine a little further how this outcome fared much better than my average seven-day progression. Positive thinking is great, but that's just *thinking*. Acting positively is, at the very least, equally as good as thinking that way, and perhaps - in many situations - even better. But I really believe the secret here is the talking out loud piece. Never before had I utilized speaking out loud, forcing myself to *pretend* to be positive while talking with a purpose, to boost others' moods. Being on camera does indeed add more pressure, but the results are greatly improved—and you haven't wasted seven days of your life.

This prompted me to reflect on one of my conversations with Dan Marlow about athletic per-

---

[6] Amy Cuddy TED Talk - Fake it Till You Make it - YouTube

formance. Athletes do a lot of thinking during their performances. We train the brain to think more positively and try to visualize the intended outcome. But one day Dan said to me, "Don't just sit back and listen to the voices. You need to <u>be</u> the voice in your head. You need to control the thoughts; meaning don't wait for the thoughts to come to you; you create the thoughts. Then you say them in your head. Then, say them out loud." You'll achieve far better outcomes using this method. By creating the thoughts and then saying them out loud, you are occupying your brain with only positive thoughts and goals. There is no longer time nor room for anything but the words you are saying. You are in control of them.

When I went back inside the house, Jennifer needed only to get a glimpse of me to see that I was no longer pissed off. I would love to tell you that she came to her senses and apologized, but it didn't exactly go that way. I cannot recall who said what to whom, but I do remember that it was over. And that, in and of itself, was a relief that boosted my mood north of seven out of ten.

I was in control of my mood once again, and I had learned that sometimes my pride or selfishness gets in the way. In that argument with Jennifer, I had felt justified because I was sure I was right. I hadn't backed down, because the facts were on my side. The problem with this approach is that the opposition sees the reverse. You have your truth and they have theirs. Your perspective is based upon the view from where you sit, but they have chosen to sit somewhere else.

While teaching my daughter to drive, I gave her this piece of advice: "There will be times when you are driving and have the right of way, but another driver (who is in the wrong) could very well smash into your car if you don't yield to them. If you choose to proceed anyway with the justification of being right, your car will still be damaged, and you could both be seriously hurt. There will be police reports, insurance claims, and so on. You must take action to protect yourself."

I applied my own advice on the day of my first nosedive, and here is what I learned: you can control your mood with a few techniques to force positivity. The "fake it till you make it" practice is not limited to career opportunities or business promotions. It has the potential to be unlimited.

CHAPTER TEN

Those Negative Ninnies

Have you ever confided in a friend when you were having a problem? Shown vulnerability and opened up, hoping they might impart some wisdom to help you see a solution that you hadn't considered? And instead, they only offered, "Don't worry, it'll be okay." That kind of response makes me want to scream! My sarcastic brain wants to reply, "Wow, 'don't worry about it', I would have never thought of that gem on my own, that's was so helpful." But I keep that thought to myself. Their comment wouldn't exactly instill confidence in their ability to help me deal with a problem. Why do I mention this?

In Chapter 3, I share the 'superpower of a heightened sense of awareness' theory. Anyone dispensing the "don't worry about it" advice is not showing that capability. They may be great friends, but I sure wouldn't want them on any team of mine that requires its members to display trust, insight, and caring. I prefer to surround myself with individuals who exhibit that heightened sense of awareness, who sense when I need more than to be dismissed with a, "Don't worry about it," and a pat on the back.

***

So, we've established that I'm a dreamer. I own it; I embrace it. For whatever reason, from a very young age, I cannot recall a single time where I considered giving up on an idea instead of formulating a plan to get it done.

I am the youngest of three boys, and there was a small gap between number two and myself, as my mother miscarried at her third attempt for a daughter. Mom had always wanted a daughter, so my parents decided to try one more time, and in May of 1964, they got me instead. My mother decided to take time off from work this time and stay home with me until I was old enough to attend school. It was not until I had my own daughter that I realized the great benefit of not having to go to daycare. My mother, knowing I was her last child, wanted to enjoy every little bit of raising her baby. Her decision provided me with comfort and security—even in the late '60s there were whispers of child molestation within religious and civic organizations. Things were changing, and I was fortunate that my mom decided to keep me home. We were a family of modest means, but for the most part, we were happy.

Child-rearing strategies were changing in those days, and my parents chose to use different methods with each of us boys. My oldest brother was brought up the way children of first-time parents often are —strictly by the book. Good old Dr. Spock. Subsequently, for reasons unknown to me, the leather belt became a parenting strategy with less than favorable results.

Fortunately for me, my parents began to look inward and implemented new child-rearing strategies. Encouragement. Positive reinforcement. In 2021, it is obvious that creating an environment of support and encouragement is a sound method for child raising, but in 1970, the idea was cutting edge. No more threatening or yelling, and no more leather belt! I was praised, encouraged, and supported. I thrived in this new environment, and it showed.

I excelled in grade school and athletics. Being the youngest of three boys, I usually played with kids four to six years older than I was. It did not deter me; it inspired me to try harder. The older kids made me believe I was a good athlete too, with their frequent compliments. This worked wonders for my self-confidence.

In the early '70s, the Vietnam War was winding down; several years prior, America had put a man on the moon. The rapidly growing economy boosted spirits and wallets. A car in every garage. Positivity was everywhere you looked.

And to make matters better, although I did not know it at the time, I was a good-looking kid. Being of Italian descent on my mother's side, I had a near permanent tan. I saw it as a curse, but to my brothers' girlfriends, I was irresistibly cute. When I was in elementary school, I thought girls were icky. If I had only known! But the attention they gave me supported a positive mindset. Complements were never in short supply.

So, through my elementary school years, I always displayed a "what if" and "why not" attitude. I was naturally curious, and a true believer in optimism. With all the new advancements in science, America was riding high. Space travel, supersonic jet airplanes, medical breakthroughs; America was leading the world in scientific advancements. During my college years, the computer was being widely adopted by businesses. What an amazing time to be alive! What *couldn't* our country accomplish? With the United States being idolized around the world, how could a youngster in America *not* have a positive outlook?

Even still, there were negative ninnies. The proverbial gray cloud followed them like it did Eeyore in *Winnie the Pooh*. I didn't get it. I still don't. My mom used to say some people will cut off their nose to spite their face.

Fast forward to the prepubescence of iMOO-Divate. Those cynics, always looking to find fault, are still around. "Hey Jay, you're not in such a great mood all the time." "I saw you in a bad mood."

As a positive thinker, it shocks me when someone wants to scrap a program because of a single failure, or even a simple setback. It would be like never driving again just because of a flat tire. Flat tires have never stopped me! I change the tire and keep driving. You can count on setbacks, but you should not let them stop you.

What I say to those folks is this: "It is a good thing you didn't give up when you first tried to walk." In a 2014 study of 130 toddlers, researchers found that they fell an average of seventeen times an hour.[7] If they were new walkers, they fell sixty-nine times an hour! The babies saw everyone else walking, and they weren't going to be denied. They were determined. They *were* going to walk!

It has now become fashionable to be hypercritical and to point out others' flaws without solicitation. There's enough material there to write an entire book! But I subscribe to Finnish composer Jean Sibelius's philosophy: "Pay no attention to what the critics say; there has never been a statue erected to a critic."[8]

The world is filled with people idolized for their resiliency and success, even in the face of devastating failures. We've all heard the following examples, but they make me smile, so here you go. Thomas Edison said this about his multiple scientific failures, "I have not failed ten thousand times—I've success-

---

[7] www.veipd.org/earlyintervention/2014/01/09/toddlers-weeble-wobble-and-fall-down-when-is-it-cause-for-concern/
[8] www.forbes.com/quotes/4904/

fully found ten thousand ways that will not work."[9] J.K. Rowling was turned down by a dozen publishers before Harry Potter became a household name.[10] Oprah Winfrey was fired from her first television job as an anchor in Baltimore.[11] Elvis Presley failed music class.[12] Albert Einstein's speech was delayed, and at one time he was considered handicapped.[13] The list goes on. What is important to remember is that each failure fueled the future successes of these people. There will always be cynics to take pleasure in others' failures, as it helps to downplay their own shortcomings.

Assess the people in your life. Are they supportive, or are they self-centered? Are they helpful, or critical? Do they take joy in your success, or in your failure? What is their place in your life, and why? Is it time to break the connection? Then do a self-assessment. Have you tapped into *your* heightened sense of

---

[9] www.smithsonianmag.com/innovation/7-epic-fails-brought-to-you-by-the-genius-mind-of-thomas-edison-180947786/

[10] www.entrepreneur.com/article/333381

[11] www.businessinsider.in/science/23-incredibly-successful-people-who-failed-at-first/slidelist/31624813.cms#slideid=31624815

[12] www.musicianguide.com/featured_biographies/pages/cmx6f6rpad/Elvis-s-Childhood-L-C-Humes-High-School.html

[13] globalteletherapy.com/the-einstein-syndrome-sometimes-language-delay-isnt-what-you-think/#:~:text=Einstein%20Syndrome%20is%20the%20term,other%20areas%20requiring%20analytical%20thought.&text=Einstein%2C%20a%20certified%20genius%2C%20was,he%20was%205%20years%20old.

awareness? Are *you* picking up on others' signals and responding, or are you a Negative Ninny?

Here's a simple litmus test for how to decide who stays or who goes in your life. Take out your cell phone. Look at the top ten people you call and text the most. If you're over forty, look at your phone 'Favorites.' Under forty, look at your Snapchat 'Most Recents.' Now, consider what <u>you</u> want from life. If money is your thing, most likely, you will be about as rich or poor as your top ten list. You'll be about as smart as your top ten. Same goes for most any other attribute you want to try to measure—including happiness and positivity. You are a product of your environment. I know that's nothing new, but now is the time to reassess, re-evaluate. Are you hanging around the right people to be where you want to be in ten years? Is it time for a change? Remember, "A year from now you'll wish you started today!"

CHAPTER ELEVEN

It's Not What's in the Cards You've Been Dealt, It's How You Play Them

"So, Jay, what's with all this positivity stuff? You're just saying a word." I've found that the universe provides. Sometimes people ask me about positivity, beyond walking into a coffee shop and telling a very unassuming, very kind server that I feel amazing. What is the risk in that? It's just a word. They want to know about the bigger stuff—the true power of positivity, which, if you think about it, should be obvious.

People with positive attitudes tend to have far more exciting experiences, and far less painful ones. They are more interesting; people want to hang out with them because they appear more approachable—they actually look more attractive because they smile more. That is an example of an obvious "surface" difference you stand to gain when you adopt a more positive attitude. And there are other things that science has proven—but are not as well known.

To reap the benefits of positivity, you must make a conscious choice. Your attitude is the *only* thing in life over which you have 100 percent control. You choose to live a positive lifestyle—or not! Whether it takes more effort for some folks than others doesn't really matter—the goal is to move the needle in a favorable direction. So here is the big deal stuff: scientific studies have proven that people with positive attitudes live longer.[14] This is pure, indisputable scientific fact. You could live longer by adopting a positive attitude. Isn't that fascinating? And not only that—but you could also live *substantially* longer by thinking and behaving more positively.

Science has also determined that you get fewer colds if you are positive [15]. When first faced with that information, I thought, how can that be? If you are exposed to a virus, you will catch a cold. Yet it has been proven beyond the shadow of a doubt.

We are not talking about narrow margins here; studies have also shown a significant decrease in some major illnesses and afflictions throughout the lives of positive-minded people, including heart disease

---

[14] August 26, 2019 - Boston University School of Medicine: *After decades of research, a new study links optimism and prolonged life. Researchers have found that individuals with greater optimism are more likely to live longer and to achieve 'exceptional longevity,' that is, living to age 85 or older.*

[15] Happy people are healthier, Ca | EurekAlert! Science News Releases

and depression.[16] The more positive you are, the less likely you are to succumb to, or even be diagnosed with those illnesses.

I have a doctor friend who speaks simply and matter-of-factly to me, in small words that I can understand. When discussing these issues with him, he essentially said the two things about human beings that we (the medical community) understand the least are the immune system and the brain. Hold on - you mean to tell me we've spent hundreds of years and trillions of dollars on medical research, are the most technologically advanced society in human history, and we don't even understand the human brain and immune system? To be fair, he did say it's what we understand *the least*. It's all relative.

What is most amazing to me—stunning, really—is that with all of this knowledge about the benefits of positivity, some people still choose to be negative. Sometimes it feels as though there is more negativity in our world now than ever before. Can we really afford to be negative? Who would want to? Case in point: I knew a man who used to come into my business—he was so well known for his negativity that we used to joke that he was only happy when he was unhappy. It made absolutely no sense to me!

Here is where I'll tell you my story—to this point only known to a handful of people, I am living

---

[16] www.mayoclinic.org/healthy-lifestyle/stress-management/in-depth/positive-thinking/art-20043950

proof of the claims that I've made and those which science has suggested.

More than twenty-five years ago, while working as an alpine ski coach, I broke my ankle. I went to an orthopedic doctor who, after fully examining me and my X-rays, stated, "You're never going to run again." "No biggie," I thought. I wasn't a runner, so I wouldn't miss it! During the recovery of my busted-up ankle, which was broken in several places, I contracted reflexive sympathetic dystrophy (RSD), a relatively rare syndrome. It's an excruciatingly painful condition that is usually quite debilitating and is a result of malfunctions in the nervous and immune systems. In my case, the pain presented as hypersensitivity, or a hyper-reaction where even the bed sheets touching my toe would feel like a spike stabbing my ankle and the surrounding area. RSD forced me to rely on crutches for the better part of a year and a half. Not fun, and I still remember it vividly—as it left a bruise on my brain. But I was determined not to let it beat me.

My persistence kicked in. Over the following five years, I managed to condition myself by establishing regular program of walking, which progressed to light jogging. I would jog one hundred yards and then go home and apply ice to my ankle. Within three years of starting this regimen, I could run a 5K—pretty remarkable considering I had never run a 5K in my life! Fast-forward to the end of my five-year regimen; I was running marathons and triathlons, and not just showing up, but occasionally on or near the podium. I had to laugh because the doctor had said I would never run again. I had systematically powered through with a positive mentality. I wonder what the result might have been if the doctor told me I'd never play the piano again? I do love the piano, but am terrible at playing it!

Oddly, though RSD is an extremely rare syndrome, a high school classmate of mine also contracted it. I was not aware of her condition because she moved away after high school and I lost contact with her. But eventually we reconnected on Facebook, and I learned of her condition. As it turns out, there are different degrees of severity for each patient. My friend had a severe case, which overtook her entire body, causing her to rely on a wheelchair. When I mentioned this to my orthopedic doctor, he commented that I was lucky—if there is such a thing as a good level of the syndrome, that is what I had.

Many years later, I was at my eye doctor's office for an exam, which included a series of routine tests. At the conclusion, he said, "Hey, have you got a minute?" He ran additional tests, checked, double-checked, and triple-checked the results before announcing, "You've got glaucoma."

Now *that* got my attention. I had images of being completely blind at the tender age of forty. But there was no way I was going to let that happen! I still had way too much living to do! When I made that clear to my doctor, he explained that there are several different types of glaucoma, including one called *pigmentary glaucoma*, which is what I had been diagnosed with. I was instructed to use prescribed eye drops to maintain the correct pressure for a period of five years. If, at the end of five years, the disease was under control, I could expect to maintain excellent vision for the rest of my life. So, of all the glaucomas out there, I had gotten the *good* kind.

I remained very positive through my medical trials, focusing on the fact that I had the *good* type of each syndrome, and how to move toward positive resolutions for both. I zeroed in on what would happen—where I wanted to be, and how I was going to get there. The way I saw it, I had no other options.

Fast forward a couple of years, and during a routine physical, my MD concluded that something was off. Tests and more tests were ordered, and it was determined that I do not have a right kidney. To make matters worse, the kidney that I *did* have was damaged from all the anti-inflammatory drugs I had taken to treat the pain and swelling of my ankle due to RSD. So, while I wished I had had two kidneys, I hoped that at least the remaining kidney would be sufficient to keep me alive and functioning properly! My doctor reassured me with this: though I was born without my right kidney, somehow my left kidney had compensated for the deficit throughout my entire life. In infancy, it began to grow. It grew, and grew, and now it was twice the size of a regular kidney; in fact, I've nicknamed it my Super Kidney! I wasn't even aware of this possibility and did nothing to correct the situation. I attribute yet another lucky bounce to my positive attitude. I joke about it with my wife and daughter, especially when I win an event. I say, "I beat 'em with one kidney tied behind my back."

How could someone have three medical near-disaster diagnoses and come out smelling like a rose each time? I would like to think it's because I'm such a good guy or just lucky, but I have to credit adopting a positive mental attitude as much and as often as humanly possible, being aware that better options always exist. Forging ahead!

Medical testing continued after my kidney diagnosis; again, my MD sensed something was amiss. He ordered an MRI of my brain, and—I think you might guess where this is going—I learned that I had a 3 mm brain tumor. "Here I go again," I thought. I gathered all the positivity I could muster as more tests were run. Want to guess what happened next? My doctor explained that this type of tumor was the *good* kind; that with minor medical treatments, I could expect to lead a normal life—normal in length and health. Mind you, *normal* isn't a word I've ever used to describe myself—it's too close to *average*, which, frankly, feels like an insult. Yet there I was being told I had a brain tumor, and it was the *good* kind to have! You know what? This time normal ain't so bad.

Have you personally known anyone facing four very different, difficult medical diagnoses in a row, only to learn they had achieved the best possible outcome? I cannot be that lucky—or can I? Maybe I did not recognize other outcomes because I'm not even looking in their direction. I'm always looking forward; praying to and focusing on the positive—as if no other options even exist.

The breadth of personal evidence that I just presented corroborates the scientific theories presented earlier. Good—no, *great* things can happen by adopting a positive mindset. Being healthier, having improved relationships, warding off depression. When people ask me how I can be so positive, I look at them and say, "How can you *not?*"

CHAPTER TWELVE

The Great Race

When I woke up the Sunday morning of the Great Race, I had no idea my life was going to change forever.

It was a beautiful, sunny day at the St. Albans Bay Town Park, where competitors tended to their equipment, buzzing around like bees. Race officials guided racers and spectators alike. Dynamic music pumped throughout the grounds, keeping pace with the activities.

I was at the park to watch a friend compete in the Ironman category. This impressive undertaking was certainly worthy of my support and admiration. I soaked in the remarkable sights and sounds and soon realized opening ceremonies had concluded. The starting gun was fired, signaling the runners' departure. It was an out-and-back run, meaning I would see all the runners a second time when they turned at the halfway point and finished the run, where the start was. I took my position with my camera in hand, with hopes of shooting a decent picture or two.

It wasn't long before all the leaders returned. The tight-knit pack at the start of the race had spread out considerably by the end of the 5K run. One by one, the runners pranced by. My friend was in the middle of the pack, which was respectable considering that he was one of the few performing in all three disciplines at this triathlon. I scurried back to the finish line to witness his transition from the running portion of the race to the twelve-mile cycling leg. He quickly geared up, and was off in a flash! I knew it would be more than a half hour before he would return to perform the final leg of this event; a three-mile canoe trip around the bay, so I watched and cheered all the other brave souls who chose to run on this great day. I was impressed! So many people left their excuses at home and chose to participate in life instead. These people didn't come to win. They came to have fun.

Everyone had their own story for being there. The last few runners appeared to be folks who were participating as a personal challenge, not to win a trophy. They dragged themselves over the finish line. The crowd clapped and cheered each person to the finish in a show of heartfelt support. I glanced back toward the final turn of the racecourse. There appeared to be one more competitor yet to cross the finish line. One by one, other spectators also looked in that direction. Who was the final runner? Was he hurt? What was his story? I wondered.

We all watched in silence as the shadowy figure got closer. His gait was unorthodox. He was slightly bent at the waist, with a bit of a limp. He pressed on as if he were injured. A very small woman pushed me aside, making her way to the front of the crowd. She was in a hurry.

Standing on the double yellow line in the center of the road, several feet ahead of the crowd, the lady placed both hands on her knees and took a deep breath. She had captured the crowd's attention. The entire crowd wondered what would happen next. "COME ON, DICK!" yelled Martha, Dick's caregiver. I couldn't believe this little woman could yell so loudly! She bent over and pulled in another deep breath. "YOU CAN DO IT!" she screamed, even louder than the first time. Whispers rippled through the captivated spectators: "That's Dick Bashaw!"

Those who knew that courageous man informed those who didn't. On Martha's third yell, a few others joined in. That was the cue the rest of us had been waiting for. The crowd cheered louder and louder. The little woman could no longer be heard over the din, but continued with her support. Dick was now within one hundred feet of the finish line. Each step looked more agonizing than the one before it. It looked as though Dick might collapse at any moment. The thunderous applause of several hundred hands erupted as a small opening split the mob in half to welcome the final runner to the finish. I broke my focus on Dick and took a look around the people near me. Obviously, I wasn't the only one struck by what I saw. There wasn't a dry eye in the house. Tears streamed down hundreds of cheeks, tears of joy and inspiration.

There was a purpose for my being there that day; I just didn't know what it was. I quietly walked away from the activity and thought about it. While processing what I had witnessed, I decided at that very moment that there was an opportunity I couldn't let slip through my fingers. But what was it?

During the awards ceremony, I watched my friend receive a trophy for competing in the Ironman category. Then I saw the winner of that category. He was ripped, suntanned, and toned. He smiled—a lot. He had cool sunglasses. Yup, man-crush. I watched in awe, as it was quite an accomplishment. Dick Bashaw presented the trophy and congratulated the athlete. Dick had been bestowed the honor of issuing all the trophies at the Great Race, which this year was his first event since his accident.

I learned on that day that many years ago, Dick was struck by a car while cycling. He had been a tremendous cyclist, one of Vermont's best. In fact, he still holds the course record for the cycling leg of the Great Race Triathlon. One wrong move by a careless driver ended his cycling career in an instant—and nearly ended his life. Dick's injuries were so severe he was not expected to survive the night of the accident. The following days of a touch-and-go prognosis turned into weeks of an induced coma, and then onto many years of therapy and rehabilitation.

As time passed, Dick's prognosis became slightly better. His doctors said that if it weren't for his amazing physical fitness, he wouldn't have made it. Through God's will and Dick's determination, he overcame astronomical odds. He made a decision to survive, and to get as much of his pre-accident life back as he possibly could. That inspired me, and I wondered, "Could I run?" I had just ditched the crutches from RSD. I quietly watched Dick hand out each and every trophy that year, and I imagined what it would be like if he handed me one, too. When you're setting goals, why settle for just *any* trophy? Why not aspire to the first-place trophy for the Ironman division? I made this pledge: If I competed and won, I'd give the first-place trophy to Dick, for inspiring me to set this goal. After all, he was the one that encouraged me to get off the sidelines.

Four years later *to the day*, I fulfilled my part of the bargain. Dick handed me the first-place award in the Triathlon Division. Not only did I win the Ironman category, but of the more than two hundred teams entered, I beat all but eight of the four-person teams. I was placed in the Championship Division and awkwardly stood solo, next to all the other four-person teams. They all looked at me as if I were there by mistake. I went home that Sunday night and reflected on the previous four years. It was amazing, to say the least.

I drove to Dick's house the following afternoon and met with him to have a short, quiet conversation. I told him how he inspired me to set a goal, and that I wanted him to have my gold medal. In retrospect, it's kind of odd—of all the trophies I've won, the one that means the most to me isn't even on my shelf. Because of the residuals of Dick's traumatic brain injury, I'm not sure he completely understood how much this meant to me. I shook his hand and thanked him. I held his hand – perhaps longer than I normally would have - and looked deeply into his eyes. I thought if my words didn't deliver the message, perhaps he would sense my energy. It's hard to fathom how much Dick's inspiration on that day has enhanced my life. I'll be forever in his debt. And paying that debt off has been nothing short of a bargain.

CHAPTER THIRTEEN

Skinning

I live in Northern Vermont. I specify the region to emphasize that winters are long, temps are cold, snow is deep, daylight is short, and, much of the year, vitamin D is scarce. I have found that the winter rolls by a little faster when I exercise, both indoors and out. Exercise not only keeps me fit, but it also keeps me sane.

As an alpine ski coach who has spent most of his ski time on Jay Peak, I will tell you that there is no bad weather, just bad preparation. You can survive outside in inhospitable conditions, and in fact, you can be comfortable—*if* you're prepared and have grit. A positive attitude is also a tremendous help.

After fifty years of skiing downhill, I decided to try alpine touring (AT), a style of backcountry skiing. It requires special, lightweight equipment that allows the heels of your bindings to release for climbing; your boots have an unlock feature for extra flex to bolster climbing. The term *skinning* comes from the synthetic material that simulates moleskin. AT skiers put it on the bottom of their skis to provide enough traction to climb uphill. It gives you the ability to glide when you want to and sticks just enough to allow you to change direction.

Climbing uphill while wearing alpine ski gear is difficult, yet I find it oddly appealing. I recall the first time I witnessed skinning. I watched a man skinning up the side of a race hill and thought it was the stupidest thing I had ever seen. Ten years later, it has become my favorite wintertime sport. I am passionate about it, and I incorporate it into my weekly workouts every chance I can.

I attend spin classes on winter weekdays; weekends are reserved for skinning. Both forms of exercise push me into my target heart rate for the duration. Currently I am fifty-six years old; my maximum heart rate is 164 (to roughly find yours, subtract your age from 220). In many of my speed climbs, I hit 164 beats per minute and average 154. I live in the red zone.

Jay Peak is a skier's mountain. Known for the biggest snow and the best off-piste skiing in the east, it draws hardcore skiers from hundreds of miles away. Jay Peak's uphill policy is open to designated routes during the day.

Even on 0° days, I wear minimal clothing to speed climb to the summit. No hat, unzipped shirt. Sweat freezes on my face and hair. People skiing downhill look at me like I'm crazy—just as I had done once upon a time. To quote Tom Hanks's character Jimmy Dugan in *A League of Their Own*, "It's supposed to be hard. If it wasn't hard, everyone would do it. The hard . . . is what makes it great." iMOODivating or skinning—it's the *hard* that makes it great.

My Jay Peak record, bottom to top, is 46:30, and that's going full bore. The climb is about two miles uphill, at about two thousand feet elevation. You can imagine what it is like on top when the wind is howling. Inhospitable, and not for everyone. When the summit is closed to downhill traffic due to strong winds, uphill may still have access. At the peak, there is an eight-foot-by-ten-foot square foyer, equipped with a space heater. When you speed climb, you inevitably sweat, a lot! And when the wind is whipping, that sweat turns to ice in minutes. That could mean trouble. As long as the foyer is open and I can duck inside to strip out of my soaking-wet uphill apparel, I know I'll be okay. I use the towel I stash in my day pack to dry off, then put on thick, dry clothes for the descent.

It is exhilarating to challenge mother nature and climb in the conditions I've described. Even in less severe settings, there's an endorphin rush to make the climb. In 2021, I was on track to set new (PR) personal record in time and number of ascents, when COVID-19 took me out. Prior to this setback, I had looked for another method to reach more people to iMOODivate. I installed a small Choose-a-Mood box at the top of the mountain, inside the warming area. I taped a sheet of paper to the wall congratulating skinners on their ascent and suggesting they take a mood card. At four thousand feet, at one of the most beautiful places on Earth, it seemed fitting.

Here's' a copy of my letter on top of Jay Peak:

> I'm building an army of positivity to remove negativity in the world. It's called iMOODivate. I present to you the twelve best answers to the most asked question on planet Earth. Are you intellectually confounded? You want to know the twelve best answers, but you don't know what the question is. The question is: How are you? And I'm sad to say the most asked question on the planet is given the least amount of care and consideration. How many times have you participated in the "How are you?" "Good, and you?" mindless exchange? Millions of times. The world could use some positivity, and you can lead by example. So I challenge you. Pick a card in the area below (if they are out, I restock weekly), and for the next seven days, whenever anyone asks you the question, reply with what's on your trigger card.

It's not a big ask. It's simple, it's fun, and you might just brighten someone's day. I mean really, you just climbed to an elevation of four thousand feet. How hard could this be? You're standing on top of perhaps one of the most amazing places on Earth. It's hard to not feel incredible here. Bring the magic of Jay Peak with you on your travels. Pay it forward. The one thing you have is absolute control of your mood. Why not make it a great one? It's on you. All. You. Come back often.

CHAPTER FOURTEEN

COVID

March 19, 2021 in the middle of writing this book, it stalled. Many writers experience this, but that did not console me. Nothing sounded right. Nothing felt right. Delaying the process until the time was right was the unintended strategy. The problem is that there is never a perfect time to do anything.

For some reason I was more appreciative of being in shape this season than any year before. That is where my focus was. Each day I could see, feel, or at least log progress. As humans, that is how we measure our investments—in time, money, or energy. We look for progress. So if the book was stalled yet physical fitness was progressing, redirecting resources to the stalled activity might provide forward momentum. My manuscript was now six months overdue. It was on my mind as one of those boxes to check in the future, so that weighed on me. Unfinished business stresses me out. My concern was like a flashback to my early entrepreneurship when I was obsessed with my business. I was never off the clock. Nights, weekends, parties—I was always thinking about the business. And now, the book.

I questioned if I had what it took to write a book, even a small book like this. What propelled me was my love of the topic. I have lived it my entire life, and I've dreamed of writing a book since I was a teenager. It occurs to me now that there was never a perfect time to do it during those fifty years either. My usual inclination is to plow ahead and get it done. Sometimes it works, and sometimes it doesn't. But I was usually happier trying, even if it didn't work out. It was more satisfying than watching from the sidelines.

My performances—both in the gym and racing to the summit of Jay Peak—were nearing personal bests, which tickled me, as I'm older now, and should expect to be somewhat weaker and slower. My advancing age and injuries hampered me, but the additional challenges made my successes that much sweeter. It was midwinter, and I had logged nineteen ascents up Jay Peak. The previous winter's record was fifteen. I knew twenty was in the bag, and it was likely that I would attain something closer to thirty. Respectable for the weekender.

Daily cases of COVID were on the rise in our community. Much earlier in the pandemic, while in complete lockdown, infection rates were extremely low. During the summer of 2020, our somewhat sparsely populated county of fifty thousand went weeks with just one or even zero infections per month. I liked that math! But in late winter of 2021, variants began rearing their ugly heads, and the infection rate quickly rose. In response, we increased our precautions, both at home and at work. More diligent masking, distancing, and hand-washing. More Purell!

I was not as concerned with COVID as I might have been. My physical health was prime for a fifty-six-year-old. My cardiovascular fitness (or as I call it, my plumbing) was the best it had been since I was a young triathlete and marathoner. I was not dismissive; I figured that if I became infected, I would survive, and most likely, I would have an easier time than my fifty-six-year-old counterparts in less physical conditioned. I was wrong.

Despite the strict precautions we took at work, COVID snuck in and got us. I learned firsthand that the virus spreads like wildfire for the five days you are unknowingly infected. You have no idea that you have the virus, and neither does anyone else, yet you are highly contagious. I spend most hours of my workday in my office, alone and with the door shut. The other hour is spent grabbing lunch from the local supermarket and eating in my office or at home.

Contact tracing for COVID was implemented, and I tested negative shortly after. I hoped that my careful measures had protected me. But the following day, the fever started. Most other COVID symptoms I might have initially written off as the result of other environmental disruptions. But not a fever. I knew what had hit me, and down I went.

On days three and four, my symptoms peaked. My fever was north of 103°, and my headache was severe. I was in and out of sleep throughout, regardless of the time of day. On day five, the symptoms relaxed a bit, and I thought I was over the hump. Wrong again. The next night, COVID took a second run at me and kicked my arse again. It continued to play this cat-and-mouse game for fifteen days, to the point where I was mentally bruised. Though I did not give up, I was convinced that I didn't have much control over my recovery. I could see and feel how COVID can kill you; wear you down to a nub, both physically and mentally, until you can't recover. The horror of that thought was in the front of my mind when my eighteen-year-old asked me a couple of times each day during the last week of my infection, "Are you going to die?"

The experience reminded me of running a marathon and when hitting the twenty-mile mark, some non-runner, in an attempt to encourage, says, "Hang in there!" or "You're almost there!" Hang in there? I feel great, so how bad do I look? As a runner who always studied the course beforehand, I knew exactly how far I was from the finish line. Not so with the dreaded COVID.

So, in that vein, "Are you going to die?" I thought, "How bad do I look?" I never thought I was going to die, but if the symptoms continued for another two weeks, I would certainly start questioning when it would be over. One way or the other.

The fever lasted for fifteen days, and I was horizontal for twelve of them. It was my first experience with "blackout naps"—I had no recollection of being tired, but would wake up forty-five minutes later, wondering, "What the hell just happened?" The good news is that I never had trouble in the breathing department. My lungs were untouched by congestion. Another oddity: of the group that was most likely infected by the same "host," the two of us that are athletes were pounded the hardest. Go figure.

Spinning and skinning were swept away in an instant. I thought there might be enough winter left to recover and make another attempt to hit the twenty-ascent mark, but the snow melted, and my cardiovascular health took a hiatus. All physical attributes were swept back to zero. Start over.

During the third week of my battle with COVID, and lacking the ability to exercise, I decided to take a shot at finishing the book. The chapters I had written didn't really tell a story; they were more of a summary, almost bullet pointed. I had intended to share a story, not report the weather.

With all this extra time to think, I went back to the drawing board to see what I could accomplish. The writer's block vanished, and three years of bottled-up ideas flowed. My writing coach, Kerry, provided the perfect amount of encouragement as she read and corrected the rough draft. This book would not have happened without her. Period.

Let's be real: while my former athleticism gets a little touch of 'local glory', meaning you are known or respected in certain small groups of athletes, like in your town or county. I'm not getting any gold medals. When I am at the gym, I look in the mirror and think, "That's my competition!" It's me against *me*. Am I as good as I *think* I am; as good as I *say* I am? What *is* my limit?

Navy SEALs believe that when you've exhausted your energy to the point where you don't feel you can take another single step, there's still 40% more energy that has not been tapped into. I'm no SEAL, but I can dig down deeper. The question is, how *much* deeper? 5, 10 or maybe 15% more effort than I previously thought my max was? Tony Robbins says that we harbor self-limiting beliefs. And I agree, it's uncomfortable to push hard, but how close to the edge can one get?

During a mountain bike ride with my (then) doctor, we discussed physical performance; specifically, admiring Olympians and their super-human feats. He asked me, point blank, "Jay, do you know the difference between first place and second place?" I suggested it was the best training, coaching, equipment, meal plan etc. He said something that I will never forget. He said "The difference between first and second place is your ability to deny your body pain."

That conversation prompted me to do little things in spin class to make it more uncomfortable in an attempt to build discipline, thus improving my performance. Previously, I had set up my spin bike for what I thought was maximum performance. But in some respects, I was facilitating maximum comfort. Now, the game is to make it more *un*comfortable. I no longer allow myself a towel to wipe the seemingly endless sweat pouring off my head. I no longer allow myself to scratch or even touch my face or neck. I'm making spinning and sweating more uncomfortable, which will make other difficult things feel easier afterwards.

Having the opportunity to step into the batter's box and swing away is still a thrill for anyone questioning whether they're good enough or not. I am good enough to try, and that is all that is required in life. Sure, COVID kicked my ass, but I choose to look at it this way: it was the best thing that could have happened to me. A thirty-skin summit would not alter my life much, just another goal to try to beat the following year. Yes, a few things were stripped away from me when I was sick, but I was able to pursue other things, like writing this book. And I am 100 percent certain that when I am on my deathbed—whether next week or (as I predict) at eighty-four—my single largest regret will *not* be not having written that book.

My book copywriter cautioned me about saying COVID was the best thing that ever happened to me. I respect COVID, and I am very sympathetic with anyone who suffered any type of loss as the result of this virus. But when I hear the line "the best thing that ever happened to me," I think of Rick Yarosh.

Rick is a *hope expert* for Sweethearts and Heroes, who speaks to students alongside Tom Murphy. Graduating high school in 2000, Rick was captain of the football and wrestling teams before he enlisted in the army. On September 1, 2006, his Bradley Fighting Vehicle hit an improvised explosive device. Rick retells this story to audiences in detail, describing how he nearly died. The guy sitting next to him in the Bradley didn't survive. Rick sustained massive injuries, and was burned over 70 percent of his body. He felt his ears and nose burn off of his head. He lost his leg.

He gave up several times during the incident and during his physical recovery; and afterwards, as people treated him differently because of his looks. Most children were scared of him. He recounts the one day everything changed, because of a little seven-year-old girl in a restaurant that was curious and scared. She stood in front of Rick, staring at him. Rick said, "Hi," and she ran back to her table. Rick thought that was the end of the encounter. His life, however long it was going to be, would be a life of scaring children and feeling hopeless. Then he overheard the little girl say to her grandfather, "Grandpa, he's really nice." Rick recognized this as a spark of hope.

Soon a chance meeting with Tom Murphy and Sweethearts and Heroes led to Rick joining the team full time. He's a featured speaker, and kids flock to him. Rick is a star; a beacon of survival in the face disaster. In the face of hopelessness, he chose HOPE, "Hold On – Possibilities Exist."

Why did I bring this all up? When Rick is asked if he had a magic wand and could go back to before the incident, get his leg back, his face back, and return to his original physical appearance and athleticism, he says he would not go back. Rick thinks back to the attack and says, "It was the best thing that could have ever happened to me." Rick says if he could go back, he would not have been able to give all that hope to all those students. The lives Rick has saved with his public speaking, identifying and relating to students that were struggling with being bullied or looking different, the mail he's received thanking him for saving their lives, would never have happened. He is truly an American hero, not because of the sacrifices he made for our country, not because there is a painting of him in the Smithsonian Institute, but because of all the hope he's bestowed on so many people. Rick says he pours a bucket of hope on folks. I say God bless Rick Yarosh.

COVID also left me with a renewed sense of gratitude. And it has been scientifically documented that you cannot have a thought of gratitude *and* a negative thought at the same time.[17] So while my physical conditioning is temporarily reduced, my

---

[17] The Neuroscience of Gratitude and How It Affects Anxiety & Grief (positivepsychology.com)

mindset is still strong, still positive. I'm still looking for the good, looking for the *how can I?* This is proof that the universe provides.

CHAPTER FIFTEEN

Close of Business

I feel it is entirely natural to look back, evaluate, and monitor the direction and progress in life, and I do so frequently. It is an introspective process, an exercise in self-awareness that allows me to adapt and overcome. I look back on the moment I decided to sell my business as a pivotal time in my life.

I once owned a wholesale apparel business. It started from a failed partnership in the same industry. I had been equal partners with another fellow, or so I thought. It was a deal we had cemented with a handshake.

Our business grew quickly. We ran three shifts a day to meet orders, which far exceeded our production capacity. We got behind and bought more equipment and hired more staff to get caught up. We had hit the market perfectly, and the volume of business was staggering. I thought my ship had come in. I was onsite for at least a portion of every shift, working seven days a week, fifteen hours or more per day in order to keep the operation running. Not so for my "partner." It eventually dawned on me that this was *not* how an equal partnership works. Subsequently, by way of a very carefully crafted technical loophole, I was sidelined and ultimately forced out of the business I had poured my heart and soul into. I had not been in charge of the business checkbook and began making payroll with cash advances from my credit card. As a partner, I felt covering payroll was not a big risk, as we were certainly making large profits, but the cash was tied up in future business obligations. I did whatever it took to keep the business running. I saw the partnership one way; he saw it another. I had no leverage, and I was out.

In the fall of 1990, I left the company with $15,000 in debt, one small piece of equipment, and no form of income. I was devastated. This was a dark time for me. The takeaway? No one gives a shit about your problems, unless it's their problem too. This was a problem all my own.

What do you do when you are $15,000 in the hole, with zero income or revenue? You start a new business, of course. Somewhere along the way, my motivation to succeed kicked back in. I hustled. I worked construction during the day and at the new business by night. It was a struggle. I made the minimum payment on my credit card and obtained a rental unit for $200 a month. Food was a luxury. Looking back, I have no idea how I made ends meet.

But I did, and I am happy to say that I never screwed anyone over in the process.

My then girlfriend, Jennifer, stayed with me in the rental unit on weekends. She never complained—even when I ran noisy equipment late into the night, in what should have been the dining room. She accepted it as a necessity. A year later I moved back home and sublet two hundred square feet of commercial space in St. Albans, Vermont, to run my business. It had a desk and one small piece of production equipment. I was living at home with my mother. This didn't scream success.

Six months later, I teamed up with a talented sales rep who was thrilled with the products I was producing. This was just the break I needed. We started taking in more and more orders. I was a startup company, and I could not afford to pay workers. I simply put in the hours myself, many nights working past midnight. The Fridays and Saturday late nights were the toughest. While my friends were out partying, I was stuck working. While I was still raw from being financially eliminated from the former business, I had the drive of a pit bull. Working long hours seemed a small price to pay to succeed.

The new business started to expand. Orders steadily rolled in, and I moved into a bigger space. I got assistance from the government to hire my first employee. It was the first time in eighteen months I felt like I could catch my breath! One sales rep led to a second; one employee led to another; one customer led to another. The orders kept coming. I bought bigger and better equipment. I moved into a third building, but this time the entire space was devoted to my business, which was firing on all cylinders.

During this time, I bought a house, and Jennifer and I married. Things were going well. The industry, the sales reps, and the customers loved my work. I had never made so much money in my life.

I was back to running three shifts a day, and it was my most efficient and profitable time. We expanded again and again. When the economy took a huge dive, I zigged while everyone else zagged; I had another record year while other businesses were down 20 to 40 percent. I would love to tell you I was smart and saw it coming, but I didn't. I just went wherever the energy told me to go. Some of the local news channels came to do interviews with "the new kid on the block." I was flattered.

I had grown tired of moving from one rented commercial space to another and bought a 12,500-square-foot building on five acres of commercial property that would accommodate any future expansion for years to come. Around that time, I vividly recall my mother coming into the shop. Boxes were stacked to the ceiling; large pieces of expensive production equipment lined the floor. Staff members scurried about briskly. I saw her on one of my passes by in the rush and said hello. She stood there, mesmerized, watching traffic flow back and forth. Up until this point, she had worried that I was making T-shirts and rolling quarters for gas money. She never saw my business as a means of steady, secure income - until that day. On my second or third loop by, she stopped me, searching for the right words. "Jay Birdie, (she'd always called me Jaybird) how'd you know how to do all this?"

I replied, "You know, Ma, I'm not really sure. I just kept working and figured it out." I continued, "I guess I was just too stupid to know I *couldn't* do it!" I felt very fortunate: there I was with a successful business.

You see, I was a "blocker"—that's a local, derogatory term for someone who grew up below—or on the wrong side of—the tracks. But all I knew was hard work, and to keep going no matter what. No one outworked me; I *achieved* the blissful feeling of success. Yes, it was a team effort, but as CEO, I put it all on the line *every day*. With a little luck, a lot of sweat, and some good bounces from the universe, the possibilities were endless. My mother continued to watch and listen as the embroidery machine's needles almost created music going up and down, and staff scurried about. I finished with, "Ma, I guess if you play on Good Luck Street long enough, the Good Luck Bus will hit you." I truly felt that my success was due to luck more than anything else. I was on top of the world, and I loved it.

But it came at a cost. Jennifer and I had a child, which added another level of responsibility. I was a hands-on dad; in fact, for the first few years, I was the "bubble wrap parent" - very careful with my child, and very protective of her. Jennifer and I took turns with nightly feedings and diaper changes. I actually enjoyed it! It was quality time with my daughter. If my she had a need, I completed the task. I tracked and documented her meals. I researched the best child-raising techniques. When she was sick, I didn't sleep until she was asleep. I put all business trips on hold. My daughter was seven years old before I spent my first night away from her. It was not a sacrifice; I chose to operate this way. I didn't care what people said or what advice they gave. I did the research, chose a path, and got the desired result.

Our morning routine was stressful. As Jennifer headed out early to her teaching job I stayed home with our daughter. It took time away from the business, which I would make up later in the day or on weekends. Family time, which was in short supply, was impacted. Trips in the car were almost always interrupted by cell phone calls from employees, customers, or sales reps. There was always a question, a problem, production or sales issues. As anyone who has ever owned a business will tell you, you are never off the clock. *Never.*

Vacations were rare but much needed. We planned to take off for a week or two each year, and as our vacations approached, I left work telling myself that I *needed* this vacation; I had worked so hard that even if the entire business collapsed, caught fire, and burned to the ground, I would still go and build a new business when I returned. One week in the summer and one in the winter were more than a want: they were a need.

We traveled in style. I had accumulated countless air miles on credit cards from buying raw goods, so we always flew first class. When I was growing up, my dad drove me wherever I needed to go in a car that was multicolored (one of which was primer). Being able to offer my family some luxury was rewarding. I was proud of my achievements, but to be honest, I didn't really care for first class. All I wanted was a big chair with some legroom so I could sleep. The fanfare, I could do without. I hate valet car parking. I just feel awkward. Who do you tip, how much and when? When they take the keys, when they give it back?

Our first family trip to Disney World was emotional. As a young boy, on Sunday nights I would watch *The Wonderful World of Disney* on TV. In school, there were always a few wealthy classmates that went to Disney World. But that wasn't for families like ours. Now, standing in front of Cinderella's Castle for the first time with my wife and daughter, being able to provide for them something that my parents never had any chance of providing, I was brought to joyous tears.

After a while, the business took its toll on me. I worked an average of sixty hours a week. Over the years, Jennifer and I argued about balancing family time with business time. I had the misconception that I was irreplaceable. I could never allow even one thing to go wrong. I could not miss a single order or ship a product late. I could not let this business be taken away from me like the last one. I was always the one to take the phone calls, write the emails. The years of running the business wore me down, aged me and worsened my mood. Things that normally wouldn't bother me, did. I was short-tempered, snapped more often, and was perpetually tired. Was I irreplaceable? One day I realized as I passed by a cemetery on my way to work, that it was filled with people that thought they were irreplaceable too.

My daughter, Danielle, is my everything, and she knows it; we have a tremendous relationship. It is hard for me to imagine that anyone loves their child as much as I love mine. When she was eight years old, we took a family trip to Florida during winter break.

She and I were swimming in the pool together. I was throwing her into the water, letting her dive off my shoulders. We were like two kids playing together. I was *her* playmate, and I loved every minute of it. During our playtime, I forgot all my troubles, just for a fleeting second. At that exact moment, Danielle noticed this, looked deep into my eyes, and said, "Daddy, I love it when you're happy!" I looked back at her with a long stare, stunned.

I recalled all the times I had been unhappy. I watched a movie screen memory of my life with her over the last eight years and saw each of my mistakes, my missed opportunities. How many times had she seen me unhappy? Clearly enough to notice the contrast. It had taken an eight-year-old to make me see the difference. As the long stare into my daughter's eyes ended, I decided that I would sell the business.

IMOODIVATE

Less than an hour later, we were back in the hotel room, and I had sent an email to the business broker that had hounded me about selling several times in the past. In the past, I would not have considered it, not even for a second. But in one moment, everything changed.

CHAPTER SIXTEEN

Six Seconds a Day (and Not All at Once)

You are nearly ready to embark on an iMOODivate program of your own. You can dramatically improve your life in six seconds a day. That is not hyperbole—it *will* happen. You can even pace yourself and not commit to six seconds all at once. Take baby steps. Crawl, walk, then run!

I have given my motivational speech hundreds of times. When asked how large my audiences are, I reply that I will not speak to a group of less than one person. It's a tongue-in-cheek answer, but it is true. I have dived into a presentation with a single person. Sometimes it has been planned, and other times it's been off the cuff. If I am feeling your energy, can see that look in your eye and that smile on your face, or a look of concern—as long as the energy strikes me—I'm in.

At first, I was uneasy, but I hate being afraid of anything. So I got as close to that fearful thing as possible, stayed there, and let my intense observation skills take over - allowing me to look, listen and learn. Then, when I felt slightly more comfortable, I inched closer, until one day I was no longer fearful, and I was actually capable of helping other people.

iMOODivate requires a leap of faith. You have to put yourself out there. I have done standup comedy, and it's about as vulnerable as you can be—like being naked in public. But when you finally commit to answering the most asked question on Earth with one of the iMOODivate trigger cards, you're putting yourself out there. Whether to a stranger or friend, you are taking a risk. You could fail. It's like I told my daughter when she picked out a dress for the high school dance: "You have to own it." So, whether it's answering a question to a total stranger with "amazing" or wearing a little black dress to the dance, you must be confident in your choice. You can not hesitate; it has to be purposeful. It becomes easier as your confidence develops.

Let us break this down. I am talking about doing something that takes less than *six seconds* a day. You can do anything for six seconds. A single interaction doesn't even take that long. I will prove it to you. Imagine I'm standing next to you with a stopwatch, and take this interaction for example:

> Store clerk: How are you?
> Me" (starts stopwatch)
> You: Amazing!
> Me: (stops stopwatch)
> Time: .25 seconds

You said a powerful word in a quarter of a second! And that one word will resonate far beyond that single interaction.

There are two types of people in this world: those who dive into the water without any hesitation, and those who analyze everything. When I pitch the seven-day challenge to the first group, they throw caution to the wind. The next person they meet asks them, "How are you?" and they don't bat an eye before blurting out, without fear, "Amazing!" I find that these people are generally happy and confident and have the easiest time moving forward with the program. They smile broadly and genuinely when executing the iMOODivate program. I'm a little jealous of these types. They take action.

I partially fall into the second category—those who analyze everything. Some of these people never manage to change their robotic response to "How are you?" They will think about it for days, and if the risk of failure takes them out of their comfort zone, they won't even attempt it. For me, I analyze like crazy, minimize the risk, then try to execute the plan as though it's been written in stone.

I'd venture a rough guess that the average person will be asked how they are twenty-four times a day. With the quarter of a second that it takes to say one word, you will have the opportunity to pull off twenty-four "amazing" iMOODivate replies. You will likely be a little bit nervous, but do yourself a favor: own it, and be confident. "Hi, how are you?" Look the person who is asking straight in the eye, smile, and say one of the twelve words. "Amazing!" In the case of a shop clerk, they will most likely ask their customers how they are robotically, hundreds of times a day for months, maybe years, and *you* will be the great disrupter. A new answer in the land of monotony! You'll catch them off guard. They will smile. You'll smile back. Experts say you can dramatically improve your life by smiling.[18] Now you are both doing it—you do the math! You will have improved their day, and possibly their life. And I ask you, *why not?*

You'll play the scenario over and over in your head, and you'll feel good. You'll want more.

Here's your opportunity: take the seven-day challenge. Pick your card and "sell it" for seven days. Whenever anyone asks you how you are, face-to-face, over the phone, by text, or by social media, you must reply with what is printed on your trigger card. That is all there is to it. Then, on the eighth day, I ask that you pay it forward. Select a person that you'd like to iMOODivate and do what I've done for you. You will have graduated to *iMOODivator!*

As an iMOODivator, you will be questioned. People will hear your response and shoot back with, "Why?" This is my sweet spot. I am in my fifties, in above-average physical shape; I have a great job, a great family. I appear to have my shit together! Based on all of that, here is how I respond: "Why? I eat right, I exercise, I don't drink, I don't smoke, I don't

---

[18] bestlifeonline.com/smiling-health-benefits/

use drugs, but that's no guarantee I'll get to wake up tomorrow. I could get hit by a truck later today; I could get a call from the doctor telling me that my luck has finally run out. The guarantee of living another day is not given to anyone. So why am I amazing? ***I got to wake up this morning!***" While that answer is quite serious, within a very light-hearted program meant to be warm and fuzzy, it creates a perfect picture of what is appreciated and what is taken for granted. It's all about perspective.

I end this chapter with a plea to every reader. Take that chance. Say one word. Yes, it will be nerve-wracking for some. Your heart may race. Your face might become flush. But true happiness cannot be achieved without being vulnerable. And it's a 50-50 proposition as to who benefits more, you or the human you just disrupted. I guarantee that you will not be disappointed.

Now go do it.
Say. One. Word.

Shameless plug:
To purchase your own iMOODivate materials,
go to www.imoodivate.com

ABOUT THE AUTHOR

Jay Cummings. Born a seventh generation Vermonter on the wrong side of the tracks in a tough railroad town on the Canadian border, Cummings never let his modest beginnings discourage him from pursuing opportunities. His keen sense of observation and near obsessive competitive drive led Cummings to his best professional and personal accomplishments. Among his peers he is known for his vision, yet his family knows him as a truly dedicated husband and father to his wife and his one and only daughter. Cummings shares stories and lessons of how it took more than massive amounts of hard work and grit to succeed, citing the single biggest attribute for success and happiness is controlling your attitude. Cummings will teach you how to choose your mood through simple and effective strategies that dramatically change your mind set in an instant.

When he's not at work, Cummings relaxes as the stereotypical Vermonter might. You'll find him on the snow-capped mountains in the winter, or aboard his boat, the Genevieve (named for his wife), on Lake Champlain in the summer, always seeking new levels of clarity and awareness.

Cummings takes great pride in his 7th generation Vermonter status, with a keen ability to root out a *true* Vermonter by asking one simple question. "Lived in VT yer whole life?" True Vermonter answer: "Not yet, I haven't".

Made in the USA
Middletown, DE
12 February 2023